Learning on Your Doorste

As the Forest School movement gains popularity among UK educators, teachers are increasingly recognising the benefits of creative outdoor play. But how can busy primary school teachers fit regular, high-quality outdoor learning into an already crowded timetable? How can they plan a range of rich, imaginative and creative experiences that build up into full topics? And how can they translate the excitement and engagement that they find outdoors into increased enthusiasm and attainment indoors?

Learning on Your Doorstep integrates creative outdoor play with curricular attainment, while increasing the challenge, enjoyment and professional development of the teachers using it. The book presents a series of topics that channel the children's outdoor experience into writing outcomes to reflect the current Primary Framework for Literacy. Using child-led, kinaesthetic teaching and learning techniques, each topic helps teacher and class to build an imaginary world to explore and includes:

- session plans to enable teachers to easily access relevant information;
- collaborative activities, games and drama to stimulate discussion;
- photocopiable items such as letters, imaginary maps and animal-fact jigsaws;
- optional classroom follow-up activities and a final writing task;
- tips on how to prepare and resource each session.

Guidance on adapting for different abilities and ages is also given, along with curriculum links and pedagogical rationale, to help primary teachers put creative outdoor play at the centre of the primary teaching timetable.

The ideas in this book are suitable for implementation in any school environment, using resources commonly found in the stock cupboard or home. All you will need to add is some preparation and imagination!

Isabel Hopwood-Stephens has worked as a primary school teacher in Years 1, 2 and 3. As an OCN Level 3 Forest Schools Leader, she has also run many after-school clubs and school trips specialising in Forest School activities, and explored the benefits of creative and imaginative outdoor learning on the writing performance of her classes.

Learning on Your Doorstep

Stimulating writing through creative play outdoors for ages 5–9

Isabel Hopwood-Stephens

Routledge
Taylor & Francis Group
LONDON AND NEW YORK

First published 2013
by Routledge
2 Park Square, Milton Park, Abingdon, Oxon OX14 4RN

Simultaneously published in the USA and Canada
by Routledge
711 Third Avenue, New York, NY 10017

Routledge is an imprint of the Taylor & Francis Group, an informa business

British Library Cataloguing in Publication Data
A catalogue record for this book is available from the British Library

Library of Congress Cataloging-in-Publication Data
Hopwood-Stephens, Isabel.
Learning on your doorstep : stimulating writing through creative play outdoors for ages 5–9 / Isabel Hopwood-Stephens.
p. cm.
1. English language--Composition and exercises--Study and teaching (Elementary) 2. Outdoor education. 3. Experiential learning. I. Title.
LB1576.H655 2012
372.6'044--dc23
2012017981

ISBN: 978-0-415-53682-0 (hbk)
ISBN: 978-0-415-53683-7 (pbk)
ISBN: 978-0-203-11112-3 (ebk)

Typeset in Bembo
by Keystroke, Station Road, Codsall, Wolverhampton

FSC www.fsc.org MIX Paper from responsible sources FSC® C004839

Printed and bound in Great Britain by
TJ International Ltd, Padstow, Cornwall

Contents

Acknowledgements

With thanks to Corrie for Forest Schools, Mum for the idea, Dad for the babysitting and Rob for everything else.

1 Why use the outdoors for writing?

Introduction

Welcome to this book! I hope that it provides the inspiration and guidance that you are looking for. As teachers, we can positively influence the outlook and achievements of hundreds of children. We can create safe, supportive and creative environments where learning is a voyage of discovery and enrichment. And we can introduce children to the magic of the written word, a journey that starts with sharing a favourite story and ends with fabulous worlds flowing from the tip of a pen as we create our own . . .

Except that, for some children, it's nothing like that. Writing is a halting and unrewarding process that exposes them as incompetent. Some children come to school with a seemingly innate understanding of how to write, but what can we do to help those who don't?

This book aims to explain how we can help all children to write by taking them outside to learn. It argues that putting children in an open-ended, problem-solving situation stimulates deeper concentration and learning, benefits kinaesthetic learners and gives them first-hand experience to draw upon when producing their writing. And it seeks to demonstrate that this can be done in a typical school setting with nothing more than some planning, the contents of an average resources cupboard and a dash of imagination.

The benefits of learning outdoors

So why choose the outdoors as a setting for learning when we have perfectly well-heated and well-lit classrooms? The short answer is: because they love it. The longer answer takes in a slew of research into health, cognitive and social benefits, the main points of which are summarised below.

Health

Children love to run, shout, climb, explore and hide. This isn't always possible in a classroom, but it is outdoors. The more time children spend outdoors, the more they engage in physical activity (Mygind, 2007), and research has shown that children who spend regular time outdoors are calmer in the classroom afterwards (Forestry Commission for Scotland, 2005). They also take less time off for illness, are better able to concentrate on their work and have lower levels of the stress hormone cortisol (Grahn *et al.*, 1997). You have probably also noticed that children don't have as much freedom to roam as we used to, perhaps because of parental fears about traffic accidents or strangers. Most adults have fond, magical childhood memories of being in the woods and having the freedom to explore and experiment (O'Brien, 2004). Providing the children in your care with regular sessions outside, during which they can explore and interact with nature, is good for them – and you.

Psychological

Behaviours that seem anti-social in a confined space filled with twenty-nine other people are perfectly acceptable outside. Being in the open air gives you a chance to shout, run, leap, throw things, dig holes, build things, hide, or fall into a quiet contemplation of listening and watching. In short: freedom. This is particularly appealing to children who find themselves regularly infringing rules within the school building. The corner of the school field or a woodland area offers the additional comforts to children of being private (no strangers or dogs) and safe (no chance of getting lost, or having to keep an eye out for cars and bikes). Offering children high-quality, regular contact with the outdoors gives them a chance to forge their own relationship with it, which in the longer term will positively affect how they share it with their offspring (O'Brien, 2004).

Cognitive

A wealth of research has been conducted in this area, which can be summarised as follows. Children who are engaged in meaningful, child-led and supported activities outdoors tend to be more relaxed and engaged, leading to a wider awareness of their surroundings and deeper processing of the learning experience (Carver, 2003; Rickinson *et al.*, 2004). This in turn leads to improved memory and recall of those experiences. They are also engaged in multi-sensory learning, which I explain further below.

Support for key learning theories

Some of the most ground-breaking theories about how children learn come to life before your eyes when teaching and learning outdoors. I have summarised how three of them work below, with specific reference to outdoor learning.

Experiential learning

In essence, experiential learning is learning by doing (Dewey, 1938). By way of an example, imagine that your class is studying settings in Literacy. Your class will be using a house in the woods as the setting for a story later in the week, so you want to prepare them with ideas for description. You read them *Stickman* by Julia Donaldson. Your class could look at the pictures together in the book and discuss what Stickman's house is built from; or you could take your class outside to try to build their own houses for Stickman, from whatever they can find. Which of these learning experiences is the most powerful?

With the first scenario, the usual children who have auditory–visual learning styles will thrive on the discussion, but those with physical–kinaesthetic learning styles will be isolated, and will day-dream or disrupt their peers. With the second scenario, all the children will share a multi-sensory experience of collecting and snapping branches, digging in the soil with a twig, or heaving a heavy stone across the ground. Without realising that they're doing it, they will be collaborating and verbalising their thoughts, advising and supporting each other; this is particularly important for the kinaesthetic learners who feel that they cannot share their expertise in the classroom. And afterwards, they can speak from a position of expertise about how they built their shelter, what features it has, and even relate their experience of building it to the possible experiences of the story character. Such is the power of experiential learning.

Multiple intelligences

I have already touched upon the visual–auditory–kinaesthetic (VAK) model of learning and the problems encountered by kinaesthetic learners in a classroom environment. As children move up through Key Stage 1 into Key Stage 2, the learning styles best served by standard classroom activities tend to be visual or auditory, serving children who find it relatively easy to listen, follow instructions and imitate. So far, so disadvantageous for the kinaesthetic learner.

Gardner's theory of multiple intelligences (Gardner, 1993) takes VAK learning styles a step further, arguing that in fact we all possess eight different intelligences:

- bodily–kinaesthetic
- linguistic
- musical
- spatial
- naturalist
- logical–mathematical
- intrapersonal
- interpersonal.

He contends that some are innate to us and relate to areas where we excel, and some do not come so naturally but can be developed with support. Gardner argues that we should seek to recognise and enrich all of these intelligences, rather than using assessment and grading techniques that favour linguistic and logical–mathematical intelligences to the detriment of valuing and developing the others. Reflecting on a list of typical classroom activities in Key Stage 1 and lower Key Stage 2 – completing a worksheet, watching a video clip, listening to a story, group discussion, creating a mind-map, writing notes on whiteboards – it is quite shocking when we see the narrow range of intelligences catered for by them.

Now compare this to building a den for Stickman's family outside. The only intelligence not explicitly catered for by this activity is musical, although finding and creating sounds and musical instruments outside is a topic in its own right. There are clear organisational and assessment advantages to whole-class activities based on writing and recording, but we must not neglect the wider, richer learning experience which should feed into these.

Kinaesthetic learning

Kinaesthetic learners – those who learn by making, building, manipulating, dismantling or just fiddling – benefit hugely from activities where they have the opportunity to explore and learn at first hand. It is not always possible to accommodate this in the classroom, and neither should we seek to replace all activities which kinaesthetic learners find hard; they will still need to develop their mastery of writing and it would be a dereliction of duty to prevent them from doing so. Rather, we should be increasing the amount and quality of kinaesthetic learning experiences that they participate in, as a way of increasing their engagement and sense of expertise in the topic before asking them to write about it at length. Or, in other words, giving them a good run-up before asking them to jump the bar.

What effective outdoor learning looks like

Some of you, with fresh memories of peeling little Johnny off the fence during a previous foray into 'outdoor learning', might be reading this with a raised eyebrow. And it's true that you won't automatically enhance and enrich the learning experience by simply going outside for a while (Rickinson *et al.*, 2004). So what does an effective outdoor learning session look like?

Green space

This can be the hedges and grass in the corner of the school field, a strip of grass and shrubs behind a classroom block, or a wild area that you have planted. But most importantly, it's not the playground or the classroom. The children are able to explore and interact with the natural environment and are actively encouraged to do so.

Problem solving

Investigating a problem, where there is no fixed answer or fixed way of finding a solution, puts the children in charge of their learning and encourages them to explore their own ideas rather than worry about whether they're getting it right. Instead of passive learning, effective outdoor learning actively engages the children in looking for a solution to a problem.

Creative

Anna Craft, a leading thinker on creative learning for children, defines creativity as using a combination of imagination, intelligence, self-creation and self-expression (Craft, 2001). Put bluntly, an effective outdoor learning session should encourage these attributes in spades. The children will be invited to develop their own ideas and test out their own theories, rather than the teacher modelling something and then asking them to copy it.

Collaborative

Activities are designed to encourage team-work, pair-work and collaboration. This creates a supportive atmosphere for those easily discouraged, encourages a deeper learning experience through sustained collaborative thinking (Waller, 2007) and lets children learn socially – by talking, sharing ideas and articulating their thoughts. Teachers restrict the amount of children's speech within the classroom for understandable reasons, but we should not forget how essential it is to children's active construction of their understanding of the world (Vygotsky, 1978) and should provide meaningful, collaborative opportunities to enhance their learning.

Reflective

An effective outdoor learning experience gives the children a chance to reflect on what they have done, be it through taking their peers on a 'tour' around what they have built, or talking with their partner about what they learned today. Reflecting on what we have achieved or learned, through adversity as well as triumph, is a key learning skill that makes us more resilient and effective learners (Claxton, 2002).

Social

As already discussed, children learn by actively constructing their knowledge from interactions with their surroundings and each other. The value of talk for learning is enshrined in the Speaking and Listening objectives within the Primary Literacy Strategy (Department for Education and Skills, 2006) and the use of talk partners or learning buddies to help children absorb and articulate what they are learning. Why should this be any different outside? An effective outdoor learning session is full of children learning through social interaction: yelling across the activity area, crouched and whispering, giving instructions, listening intently, reading non-verbal cues, offering encouragement, asking questions or expressing opinions.

Tailored

We all know the pitfalls of setting a task that is too complex. The same applies here. The activities in an effective outdoor learning experience need to be accessible to all while being sufficiently open ended to provide a challenge for kinaesthetic–spatial learners.

These are the ingredients of a good outdoor learning experience, and this recipe is used for all the learning topics in the book.

So how does this all link to writing?

Researchers into writing development agree that it is a complex process, requiring a child who is writing a story to move between planning, monitoring, production and revision (Bereiter and Scardamalia, 1987), often several times and in no specific order, while composing one piece. This can make writing a disjointed process, full of stops and starts, for a child who has yet to master it. A child's willingness to pick up a pencil can also be affected by their internal view of their capability and expertise as a writer, the extent of their cognitive development, their motivation for the task and the educational context within which it takes place (Scheuer *et al.*, 2006). In other words, a child's belief about their ability and suitability to the task can affect their output as much as their mechanical skills:

> Low confidence or self-esteem is one of the most controlling elements of a child's ability to learn and behave appropriately, and thus achieve his/her own potential.
>
> (Margerison, 1996, p.176)

Another factor affecting writing is whether the child has a repertoire of default story types to draw upon. These are often absorbed through listening to stories read by adults or siblings, and their own developing reading ability (Corbett, 2008). Children who are not read to at home and who have poor reading skills are left at an obvious disadvantage here, and in greater need of an alternative means to access stories and learn the generic structures. It follows that the more actively these children are involved in the narrative of an unfolding story, the more they can draw upon their first-hand experiences to retell it or reuse its structure to their own ends.

Thus, when a child sits down to write a story they need not only to master the motor skills required to produce legible letters and words, but also to activate a memorised bank of story structures, employ learning skills that allow them to plan, review and amend their work, and perceive themselves as being up to the job in the first place. Considering the scope for failure in this seemingly simple task for an unconfident writer, it is not surprising that most classrooms contain children who will do anything to avoid writing.

Experiential, kinaesthetic, creative learning through play means that these children can explore ideas to see whether something exists or could be true (Waite, 2007). Children who do not have a mental bank of story types or well-developed reading skills can inhabit the experiences of their characters and explore the setting for the story, using drama to rehearse their ideas. Interestingly, Pie Corbett's National Strategy guidance on teaching storytelling to Key Stage 1 pupils notes the usefulness of drama for helping children generate new ideas for their writing. It also states:

> We must not lose sight of the idea that stories are experiences – not just vehicles for learning language.
>
> (Corbett, 2008, p. 3)

Is this the same as Forest School?

You may well have heard of the Forest School movement, and be wondering how it relates to using the outdoors to improve writing outcomes. Forest School is an educational concept with its origins in Sweden. Set up in the post-war era to ensure that children learned practical skills alongside an appreciation of nature, it combined the adventures of fictional characters with hands-on problem-solving activities for the children. These would include exploring and interacting with their surroundings to build shelters, find food sources, prepare food over a camp fire and use hand-tools to make basic structures and simple objects. Great emphasis was placed on collaborative working to solve problems and on the communal aspects of being in the woods, such as eating together, telling stories and singing songs.

The Forest School concept has since spread to other countries, including Japan, Russia, Finland, Latvia, Norway and Denmark, where its impact on literacy, numeracy and logical-thinking skills is valued alongside its contribution to children's social, emotional and personal development (Williams-Siegfredsen, 2005). At the time of writing it has been adopted in the UK by educational authorities in Shropshire, Wolverhampton, Gloucestershire and South Yorkshire and by the governments of Scotland and Wales.

It is highly valued for the positive impact that regular, carefully structured sessions outdoors have upon the personal, social and emotional development of children (Murray and O'Brien, 2005), including building self-esteem, self-confidence and perseverance (Rickinson *et al.*, 2004), which in turn helps children who might be disruptive to concentrate in the classroom. Forest School training for practitioners emphasises whole-child development, which means that activities and sessions must be designed to appeal to a range of learning styles and intelligences, thus allowing each child to broaden their experiences, understanding and confidence across the full range over time.

Successful pilots have been run to encourage speech and language development in Foundation Stage children (Pilsbury, 2008) and to enhance the vocabulary used in assessed writing for Year 5 children (Dismore and Bailey, 2005). Forest School-style activity has also been successfully used as an intervention for children who have been excluded from local authority education, due to persistent behavioural problems.

The specific emphasis and ethos of each Forest School setting will vary with the pedagogical philosophy of the founding members, but a typical Forest School session might be half to a whole day in duration and be based in a wooded area a short minibus drive from school. Food might be cooked on the site, over a fire, and the children will be involved in activities such as preparation and clearing up afterwards. Activities will be child led, creative and based on the children's learning schemas, as noted by the practitioners. Children will also be trained in using hand-tools and have access to them during activities to use as they wish. They will be encouraged to explore and to take calculated risks in a supportive environment, trying out activities that might be outside of their comfort zone and working with children outside of their school-based friendship groups. Above all, they will be encouraged to trust their judgement on matters, rather than seeking validation from their peers or an adult figure.

It was my training as a Forest School Leader that opened my eyes to the contribution that the Forest School approach could make to improving my relationships with children displaying challenging behaviour and then questioning the assumptions that I had made about their potential. It also pointed to the possibility of building the ethos of Forest School learning into curricular teaching. Thus, the pedagogical approach outlined in this book is not pure Forest School, but it borrows its theoretical underpinning from it. No specialist training is required to administer it, just enthusiasm and a desire to unlock the learning potential of all the children in your class.

What I found with my research

My Master's research was designed to formally evaluate something that I had noticed anecdotally when taking my classes outside to learn. My Year 2 class had been following a drama topic where a wizard had contacted us and asked for help to investigate a problem. Each session, we would find a new letter from the wizard, read it and head outside to investigate whatever he suggested. The activities were largely drama based, and afterwards we would return to the classroom and any children who wished to update the wizard on our exploits could write him a letter. This was an optional activity, and the children who didn't want to write could use the book corner. Without fail, the children who struggled with their writing and typically avoided it at all costs would painstakingly write a letter, full of ambitious vocabulary and pictures. These children had low reading levels and were all boys.

I wanted to formalise this accidental discovery through my research and see what impact a carefully planned series of sessions outside would have on a final piece of writing for low-achieving writers. Would the stories be longer, or more complete than usual? And with an eye to improving outcomes for low-achieving writers, would the final piece of writing be of a higher grade than their typical attainment level?

I devised the Enchanted Forest topic – Topic 1 in this book – featuring a boy and a girl lost in a strange wood. We were alerted to their plight via a mysterious letter delivered by an owl, and over five sessions we helped them to solve the problems they encountered by investigating them and offering advice, such as how to build a warm and cosy shelter, or how to hide their food from bears. The final task the children performed for their imaginary friends was to write them stories to read while they hid in a cave.

Out of a class of thirty, eleven of the children were writing at least two sub-levels below the government target for their year group. All of these eleven children were significantly behind with their reading, and nine of them were in receipt of free school meals. Most found it hard to concentrate and one had an individual education plan (IEP) to help manage challenging behaviour.

The results were very exciting. In summary, all of the children I was monitoring performed better in the final writing sample, producing longer, better-structured and more complete work. One child, who wrote a five-word sentence for her baseline writing sample, produced a thirty-five word story for her final piece. Two more wrote triple the amount that they had produced initially, taking their work from one sprawling, long sentence to a simple, structured story with a beginning and an end. All children produced work that was at least one sub-level higher than their typical attainment level.

And it wasn't just the final writing that was encouraging to me as a teacher. In between sessions, they would approach me in the corridor, holding out feathers that they thought might belong to the owl. Were there any more letters for us? Did I know when the lost children would write again? On playground duty, I noticed them playing games based on the activities we had completed outdoors, and over the course of the topic I noticed that all of the children started to try to communicate with the story characters through writing. Some dictated letters to the teaching assistant and then painstakingly copied them from a mini-whiteboard, others attempted it independently. The children's views of writing seemed to shift over the course of the topic too, so that during interviews with them afterwards I recorded comments such as: 'look how much writing I wrote – I never done that much writing before and I never done as much for my story before' (Hopwood, 2011).

Their enjoyment, enthusiasm and pride were gratifying. The implications for my teaching practice were clear and could be summarised thus: learning outdoors works. Get them out, investigating and exploring, and make the writing outcome part of the topic.

What about the children who can already write?

Ah, but what about the high achievers in your class – the children who already write well? What happens to them during this focus on the less able writers? They benefit too, not just from the experiential learning, but also from having the opportunity to explore and interact with their surroundings in a way that might be new to them. Children with very structured time outside of school – ballet lessons, Beavers, swimming – may not have that much time left for messing around in the woods. Children who are very able academically might initially find the outdoor topics quite discomfiting, as their spatial, bodily–kinaesthetic and naturalist intelligences may not be as well developed as their ability to read, write and calculate. It is a different experience for them to see children who usually struggle in a traditional classroom environment now buzzing with ideas and know-how, and it takes them out of their comfort zone; but it also broadens the scope of their learning experience, and puts them in a more social and collaborative learning context.

Outdoor learning works. And, as teachers, we already have the requisite skills to provide high-quality experiential learning experiences to engage our classes and stimulate their writing. This book provides six topics to stoke the enthusiasm and understanding of your class, each over five sessions, building to a clear writing outcome that is linked to the subject. The framework is easy to follow or to adapt to the needs of your class, and the resources are straightforward enough to assemble during a lunchtime (teacher's sandwich included), with the occasional prop brought in from home. All of the topics have been created according to the characteristics of effective outdoor learning outlined earlier in this chapter, and all are underpinned by the whole-child development ethos of the Forest School movement.

The rest of this book

The aim of **Chapter 2, Getting ready**, is to provide guidance on aspects of transferring your teaching to the outdoors which might catch you unawares. It includes advice on choosing the area to use, preparation of the site and resources, getting teaching assistants or other adult helpers involved, behaviour management, safety and assessing risk.

Chapter 3: How to use the writing topics

This chapter introduces the topic and session format, providing a rationale for the topic and session structure and activities. It also contains tips on making the writing outcome feel like part of the topic, and offers advice on getting involved with the storyline in order to increase the engagement and enjoyment of your class.

Chapters 4 to 9 (the writing topics)

These chapters contain six topics, one per chapter, each divided into five sessions. A summary of each topic's seasonal suitability and final writing focus is provided for easy reference on the topic introduction pages for each chapter. A table summarising these can be found in Chapter 3 (see page 24).

Chapter 10: How do I . . .?

This chapter provides guidance on items mentioned in the topic chapters, such as tips for using ICT to prepare materials for the sessions, rules for games and other activities. It also includes some pointers for teachers keen to enhance their outdoor areas, purchase equipment, apply for funding or find out more about Forest School training.

Appendices

This is where you can find all the resources referenced in the topics, such as letters from characters, maps or jigsaws, for copying and use. Please feel free to use, adapt or ignore, as you feel appropriate.

References

This section provides a list of the references mentioned in the book.

2 Getting ready

This chapter discusses choosing a site to use, safety issues and assessing risk. It also touches on resource preparation, inclusion, getting your teaching assistant on board and behaviour-management tips.

Choosing your area

Terrain

The outside space of each school is different, but what you are looking for is an area that is at least partly grassy, with bushes, trees or shrubs growing within it or along one or more of the edges. Choosing an area with plenty of green stuff is important because the children will use the leaves, sticks, stones, soil and so on for making things, and you will also want to use the same resources for hiding and hanging things. A range of plant types will give different-shaped and coloured leaf litter, and also provide a mix of autumn colours and stages of spring growth. Don't worry if the grass seems overgrown or full of weeds – the children will use the flowers and leaves anyway. Lumpy and uneven ground, steep in places, will be enormously popular with children – even if it worries you! Don't forget that you can set clear expectations about how the children move around the site, and designate some or all of it 'walking only'.

Size

On the assumption that you will be taking your whole class out with you, you need an area big enough for them to spread out without *too* much squabbling over sticks. If you are lucky enough to have expansive grounds, ensure that the area you have designated for activities is clear to the children. If your space is very limited, you could consider taking your class out in two groups, half at a time, while a teaching assistant oversees work for the remainder in the classroom, or takes the rest for an outdoor PE lesson nearby.

Location

We would all like to have access to a secret, sun-dappled glade, hidden from the school buildings. In reality though, the children need far less than that to fire their imaginations. Don't worry if the school looms large in the background, or if the area you have found behind the kitchen block seems a little dull. The children will follow your lead, and if you are excited and enthusiastic they will need little encouragement to race off with their ideas and imaginations. Walk around the edge of your school's boundary. Where are the secret corners? Where are the trees and bushes that the children could crawl under or hide in? Watch the movement of children during playground duty to work out which areas are popular with them for playing and hiding. Is there an area of the grounds that is seldom used?

One of the best areas I have found was a grassy slope with a few trees, behind the infant school block, which was covered in daisies and edged with thick privet and hawthorn hedges. Even though we could see our classroom from there, it felt secret and exciting for the children to explore this different zone. Due to recently completed building work, the area had been fenced off and now that we had access again, it had been totally forgotten by everyone.

Sister schools and local parks

If you cannot find anywhere that seems suitable, perhaps you have a pre-school, infant or junior school linked to yours? It might have facilities which you could arrange to use at a fixed time each week, and your class could present it with thank-you letters or an activity scrapbook afterwards.

Alternatively, look at a street map for the area around your school and investigate any green space within walking distance. Contact your local parks authority and ask for permission to use the site regularly. You can also ask about ranger services, such as providing access if the gate is locked, having your site checked for litter prior to your visit and the possibility of extra natural resources, such as branches and wood, being brought over to the site for use by the children.

Site preparation

When choosing your site, be wary of the following things:

Nettles: A few here and there will not be a problem, as long as you tell the children not to touch them. However, if there is a large bed, pull them up, wearing a pair of gardening gloves, and keep an eye on the regrowth.

Brambles: Again, a sprinkling of brambles is not a problem if you warn the children about thorns on the stems and undersides of leaves. If they have enjoyed untrammelled growth, however, and are particularly thick, with nasty-looking thorns, cut them back with a pair of secateurs or loppers. Do not keep the off-cuts for use on the site.

Wasps: Check with your caretaker as to whether the area has ever been treated for wasps' nests; one site I used had wild plum trees, which left the area unusable during late summer while the fruit rotted and the wasps piled in. If the caretaker doesn't know, the children certainly will; the day that so-and-so in Year 6 ran screaming across the field with a wasp in his hair will become the stuff of legend!

Ant hills: These will be no fun at all to tread in, or sink curious hands into. If you find ant hills but cannot choose another area, try to keep them at the edge of your site, and clearly show the children where they are, explaining not to touch them.

Ponds: An open pond is not a wise thing to include in an area that children will be exploring. At best, someone will be egged on to jump in; at worst, they will fall in and inhale water. Leave this resource for closely supervised use, such as pond-dipping.

Once you have dealt with any nettle or bramble growth that will hamper the children's use of the site, do a thorough litter-pick for rubbish, including broken glass and sharps. (Some school grounds are entered surreptitiously via the perimeter fence and used during the night. If this is the case with your area, it doesn't mean that you can't use it, but it does mean that you will need to check the site over, before the children arrive, for unwanted or dangerous litter.)

Risk assessment

Hey, come back! Do it once, and do it properly, and we won't need to talk about this again. A suggested template for your risk assessment is given in Appendix 1, but, broadly speaking, you will need to consider the following:

- access to and from the site (if outside the school grounds)
- moving around the site safely
- canopy level, e.g. low-hanging branches, dead branches waiting to fall
- scrub level, e.g. thorny bushes, tree stumps
- ground level, e.g. tree roots, slippery patches, uneven ground, protruding rocks
- generic activities such as gathering materials, making holes in the soil, hiding and finding things, using scissors, maintaining hygiene (e.g. washing hands after each session, no eating or putting things in mouths during the session)
- first aid provision for simple injuries such as cuts and stings, and a named first aider and procedure if something more serious happens, e.g. concussion
- names of children in your class who have epipens or inhalers to manage a condition, and where they are stored in the event that they need fetching. Alternatively, bring them out each time with a simple first aid kit. If one of your children is diabetic, ensure that the timeslot for being outside does not clash with their snacks to regulate blood-sugar levels.

Safety

Most of your safety concerns will have been addressed through your risk assessment, site preparation and behaviour management strategies (see further on in this chapter). However, you will need someone on hand who is trained in first aid, in the unlikely event of an accident. If you or your teaching assistant are not trained, check with the office to ensure that there is someone in school able to administer it while your sessions are running. It also won't do any harm to familiarise yourself with basic first aid advice available online for cuts, slips, trips and sprains.

Using an external site

If you have chosen a site outside of your school grounds, you will need to contact the owners and check their requirements for risk-assessment documentation.

You will also need to ensure that the possible risk of a serious incident (such as a dog bite, or a child handling dangerous litter) does not outweigh the benefits of the planned activities, and be clear about the school's liability for any incidents or accidents that might occur during your use of the site.

A qualified first aider will need to accompany you and you will also need to take any medication that the children have at school for emergencies, such as inhalers and epipens. Check that the number of adults accompanying your class complies with guidelines for the adult-to-child ratio for school trips.

Your class assesses the risks

If you have apocalyptic visions of your class charging around the site upon its first use, try introducing them to it before the first session. Sit them down along the edge of the area and explain that this is an area we will be using for our learning. Ask them for ideas of the kinds of things they might need to look out for – protruding tree roots, low branches, holes – and enlist two children at a time to go and tie a crepe-paper strip to anything that they think might be hazardous. Eventually, your whole class will be asked to walk carefully around the site, noting where the hazards are. At the beginning of the first proper session outdoors, ask your class to remind each other of the care they will need to take around the site.

Use of hand-tools

Due to the variable levels of experience and training in using hand-tools that there will be among this book's audience, I have deliberately omitted them.

If you have sufficient training and a high-enough adult-to-child ratio to safely incorporate their use into a session – I would suggest 1:4 for younger children and 1:6 for older children – complete a separate risk assessment for each tool. Include transport of items to and from the site, appropriate use and storage, all planned uses, and ensure that you carry appropriate first aid equipment to the site.

Perhaps most importantly, drill all the adults working with your class in the way that **you** want them to introduce the tool, model its use and then store it afterwards. Explain clearly the importance of the children's learning one safe way of using the tool and do not accept any 'gung ho' posturing from them in front of your class.

Access for children with special needs

I have worked outside with children with impaired vision and limited independent movement, and they all got stuck in, even if the adults supporting them were a little nervous.

It would be thoughtless, however, to ignore the different access needs they might have for reaching the site or being able to fully explore certain parts of it, and any issues identified should be listed on your risk assessment, with clear procedures for ensuring access. If they usually use a walking frame or crutches, the way that they need to move around the site might necessarily be different, such as crawling or rolling. Bear this in mind when checking how muddy the site is before use.

Make sure that the adult supporting the child is familiar with any procedures for the child gaining access to and using the site, and then do whatever you need to do to ensure that they are comfortable with the idea of the child being involved. Their encouragement and confidence will help that child to enjoy the challenge and difference of moving around an uneven and surprising terrain. If necessary, discuss the planned activities with the parents to secure their child's participation, explaining the benefits and enjoyment to be derived.

Keep inclusion and access at the front of your mind when reviewing the session plans, because it's important that all the children in your class feel as though this outdoor experience belongs to them. If a child has limited movement or uses a wheelchair, let them set off before the rest of the class so that they are not always arriving after everyone else has started. They could be given something simple to set up with their supporting adult, or something to look out for or find, such as the latest letter.

Resources

Natural resources

By this, I mean leaves, sticks, twigs, branches, logs, flowers, weeds, gravel, mud, berries, old bricks, leaf mould, stones and anything else that comes to hand outside. If you have an activity looming that might need more material than you think is available, you could bring in gardening waste from home, or drag stuff from different areas of your school grounds to the site for use. Ask your caretaker when the hedges are trimmed, and arrange to collect the off-cuts and transport them to your activity area. If your council runs a green waste collection scheme, nobble a neighbour and ask if you could empty some of their off-cuts into your car for use at school. Yes, they'll think you're mad, but you could end up with exotic and unusual materials like fern fronds or banana palm leaves in your site. Check any donations over carefully for thorns, nettles or anything else that you think might hurt a child's hands. If you are not sure, don't take it. Let your colleagues know that they can bring in their pruning waste and decrepit spider plants, too. State very clearly that you are looking for soft, leafy trimmings or branches; and once again, check over any donations carefully. Discard thorny, spiky or otherwise dubious materials.

Classroom resources

Find some space on a display board to create a 'woodland wall'. This will make an explicit link between the children's experiences outside and their learning indoors, bringing memories of what they have done and discovered back into the classroom. Include things such as photos of them outdoors, artefacts the children have made, items brought in by the children, and letters, maps or pictures from the topic. This will serve as an *aide-mémoire* of what your class has done so far – very useful if you run your sessions once a week and some children miss a session – and reinforce the sense that the children are actively engaged in an ongoing and developing project.

Session resources

Each session plan lists any resources that need to be copied from the appendices, such as introductory letters or maps, and you are free to copy these directly or use them as the basis for creating your own. The session plan will also indicate what further resources are to be provided by the teacher, such as string, scissors, glue or simple props. Most can be commonly found in a school stock cupboard, but make sure that you scan the plan the night before, so that you have time to dig out the more esoteric items at home.

All sessions will require some fiddling around outside prior to the start – hiding things, hanging things, sticking pictures to trees – which you or another adult will need to complete. To maintain a sense of surprise, avoid doing this in view of your class; claim a quick meeting with the head teacher and leave your teaching assistant in charge of getting their coats on and lining them up, or send the teaching assistant out with detailed instructions to set things up. As a rule of thumb, build time for preparing resources and setting up the site into your planning for each session.

Getting your teaching assistant involved

Most class teachers are supported for part of the teaching timetable by a teaching assistant, and you will certainly be glad of an extra pair of hands when outdoors with your class. The involvement of your teaching assistant is crucial to the success of your outdoor topics, as children who are unsure about what to do will take their cue from their behaviour (and yours, so remember to smile!). In a best-case scenario, the teaching assistant for your class is doing what she or he does best, supporting a statemented child or working with a group to encourage and keep them on task. In the worst-case scenario, your teaching assistant is huddled on the boundary with a sulking child tucked under each wing, glaring balefully and making pointed comments about the cold.

The more confident and convinced they are about why the class is outdoors, the better they are able to do their job. So talk to them, and seek their views. They might already be involved with the local Brownies or Cubs, and have plenty of ideas to share. They might be broadly in favour, but have reservations about the behaviour management of particular children, in which case you will need to agree a procedure for dealing with this (see 'Behaviour management' section further on in this chapter). They might have one-to-one responsibility for a child with physical or sensory impairments, and simply be worried about their getting hurt.

Knowing that the parents are in favour may stop them worrying so much, so a quick meeting after school between you, the teaching assistant and a parent will help to allay their fears – the parents may also be able to offer tips and techniques to help, or volunteer to come and help during the first session.

On the other hand, your teaching assistant's reluctance might be due to mobility and health concerns of their own that make access and involvement difficult. If this is the case, see if they are amenable to swapping with another, more able-bodied teaching assistant for the session, or enlist a regular parent helper to kneel down with the children, while the teaching assistant offers encouragement and helps to organise resources from the sidelines.

The list below is not exhaustive, but indicates the range of tasks you might want your teaching assistant to be involved with. Think about which of these you would like them to undertake, and then discuss with them:

- one-to-one support for a statemented child
- one-to-one support for a child with sensory or physical impairments

- inclusion support for a pair or small group of children
- setting up the site prior to session
- collecting in any resources after session
- bringing up the rear on the way out/way in
- going ahead with a particular child or group on the way out/way in
- handing out and collecting in resources
- moving about the site to offer help as required
- dressing up as a character
- hiding behind a bush or tree to provide sound effects/leap out suddenly
- taking an active role, e.g. as a team leader, organising groups
- supervising an activity for children who have finished the main task early.

You will know whether your teaching assistant prefers to work quietly with children or enjoys a more public role. The golden rule is: don't ask them to do something that they are clearly uncomfortable with.

As they discover the potential and possibilities for learning outdoors, your teaching assistant might surprise you by becoming the school's answer to Ray Mears . . . or they might try out a few sessions and dig their heels in. In this event, consider parent helpers or swapping teaching assistants with another teacher for that session.

Behaviour management

The benefits of being outside, such as the freedom to run and shout, should be reaped by your class. Your management of their behaviour must be adjusted accordingly; they should be able to move around the site freely, dropping in on other groups to talk or calling across the site to their friends. However, different rules doesn't mean no rules, and you will find that many of the techniques used indoors work outside too.

A 'woodland charter'

Behaviours such as kicking, hitting, pushing, fighting, throwing or sabotaging the work of others are unacceptable. Agree a space that can be used for five minutes' time out, and an arrangement with another teacher to send in any child who will not co-operate. As a class, compile and explain the purpose of rules specific to the outdoors, such as *no snapping branches off trees* or *no running through areas where people are working*, so that they understand the logic behind them. Make the rules for outdoor learning clear to your class by reviewing them orally at the start of a session, or listing them as a 'woodland charter' on your woodland wall in class.

Positive reinforcement and proximal praise

Try to maintain a steady flow of public praise for children moving carefully around the site, sharing things well, working well as a team or encouraging their peers. Especially single out children who might not typically be the recipients of such positive comments. Ask your teaching assistant to do the same. This will counter any of the public disciplining that you might have to do and show the children that their good efforts are noticed.

If you want to avoid sending a child for time out, try praising another child nearby who is demonstrating the desired behaviour, being sure to praise the child you are monitoring as soon as they start to do it too. This doesn't always work, but it can be an effective preventative measure.

Behaviour flash-points

In my experience, behaviour problems outside tend to occur for three reasons.

1. **Some children are very excited** and find the temptation to just rush off unbearable. Pair a child who is liable to bolt with a calmer, dominant personality who can be their learning buddy and help them to understand the task before starting, or ask your teaching assistant to keep an eye on them.
2. **The activities are pitched too high**, so your class start messing about and arguing. When looking at the session plan, feel free to tweak the activities to a level suitable for your class, or even scrap what's suggested and supply your own. No one knows your class better than you, so go with your instincts.
3. **They have finished their work early** and want something else to do. Have a list of 'tidying up' tasks that they could help with, or encourage them to roam around the site, offering help to others. Alternatively, offer praise for their work and, through open questioning such as 'I wonder if . . .?' or 'Do you think that. . .?', encourage them to come up with something else that they might want to add to it.

Some final tips

Generally, the children absolutely love being outside, and respond to it with excitement and enthusiasm. As you get used to taking your class outside, be prepared for the following:

Lots of excitement, movement and noise. The first sessions you do outside may seem incredibly noisy and chaotic if you are used to a very well-organised classroom with slick routines. If you have achieved the objectives on the session plan, the children have enjoyed it and no one ended up impaled on a stick, it was a success, no matter how noisy.

Disciplining unacceptable behaviour. Be prepared and be consistent. The quicker your class understand what is not acceptable, the less you will encounter it.

Initial reluctance to work outside friendship groups. You might find this more pronounced with younger children, but being in an unusual environment or context will draw the children back to their friendship groups. Let them get used to the outside environment before you raise the benefits of working with others, perhaps in a little discussion at the end of a session, so that they are primed for it at the next session.

Roaming children who become disruptive. Some children will find it hard to settle down with the activity, and may start wandering around, disrupting the others or complaining incessantly. Avoid this, where possible, by pairing them up with a particular child, or asking your teaching assistant to get them started. Otherwise, ask them to come with you while you move around the site offering advice, praise and encouragement. Involve them in the discussion with other children and watch carefully for signs that they are ready to settle down and start working.

A rush on your resources. If you are bringing out glue, sellotape or scissors for an activity, make sure that you have enough to cope with many simultaneous requests. The younger your class, the more support they will need with using sellotape and scissors, so bear this in mind and modify the activity as you see fit. Consider enlisting a regular parent helper if you know someone who fits the bill.

3 How to use the writing topics

This chapter explains how to use the writing topics and maximise the impact of their content, while also outlining the rationale for their structure and activities.

What is a topic?

Each of the six topics in this book is a learning topic that builds to a writing outcome. Each topic is divided into five sessions, from introducing the topic to your class to completing the writing assignment at the end. The generic structure of the sessions and the rationale underpinning them are outlined later in this chapter in the section 'What is a session?' Each topic is intended as an imaginary world that your class will enter and inhabit for the duration. The learning that they undergo within the topic will be a collaborative experience that also gives them a private bank of first-hand expertise to draw upon for the final writing outcome.

The topics in this book can be loosely linked to areas of study in the primary National Curriculum, and these links are clearly indicated on the introductory pages of each topic. However, the topics are *not* intended as a replacement for covering the learning objectives outlined in the relevant Qualification and Curriculum Development Agency planning, or equivalent. Rather, they can be used as an enhancement. Depending on the year group you are teaching, there may be no obligation to cover the curriculum content linked to these topics at all, but this does not mean that they are unsuitable for your class. Bearing in mind the age range given in the subtitle of this book, tips are given for how to simplify or extend the activities, and differentiated materials are provided in the appendices. Guidance on modifying session plans to suit the specific needs of your class is given further on in this chapter.

Topic duration

The duration of each topic can be as short as one week (one session per day for five days) or as long as five weeks (one session per week over five weeks). Alternatively, you could go for total immersion, covering all the session content in two days, although this will create quite an overhead of resource preparation! How you space the sessions out is entirely up to you and will also depend on the other demands of your teaching timetable. It's worth bearing in mind that the longer the gap between sessions, the more important the woodland wall becomes in your classroom as an *aide-mémoire* for your class to recount their adventures so far before embarking on the next part.

Topic flow

Each topic begins with the first session, and the discovery of a message for your class. This might take the form of a letter, an email or a coded message. This provides a hook to draw the children in, and also introduces them to the broad theme of the topic, such as helping to solve a crime. They will also be introduced to any characters forming part of the topic's narrative, such as two children investigating a sighting of a very rare animal. Your class will be invited to get involved straight away.

The second, third and fourth sessions will use the same communication device as the first, and will build the children's practical experiences of the topic. The fifth and final session will present the topic's writing outcome to the children, but within the context of concluding their involvement with and assistance to the topic characters.

How will I know which topic to choose?

Each topic is introduced by pages which indicate the following:

Summary: a sentence outlining the nature of the adventure, e.g. *help two children to escape from an enchanted forest by exploring solutions to their problems.*

Guidance: this gives a brief description of the topic theme and introduces any characters that will be referred to, e.g. *Carrie and Farid are two children lost in an enchanted forest.* It will indicate which narrative device introduces the topic and links up the sessions, such as letters. It will also summarise the activities involved.

Resources: an overview of requirements is given in a section called 'The basics', which also includes any appendix references. The 'Wow factor' gives a few ideas for creating additional drama and excitement. The resources listed on the topic introduction pages are all provided by the teacher. Resources provided in the appendices of this book are listed in the relevant session plans.

Writing outcome: a brief explanation of the writing assignment at the end of the topic, to allow teachers to see how it fits in with wider curriculum planning.

Follow-up activities: an activity summary indicating how these contribute to the final writing outcome.

Curricular links: given where applicable.

Author's comments: a mix of topic overview, enthusiastic pep-talk and advice to get you started.

Quick reference table for topics

One consideration for choosing a topic must be the season of the year; some of the topics are more reliant on abundant supplies of natural materials than others. You will also want to know how the writing outcome dovetails with planning in other subjects. These aspects are summarised in Table 3.1, but for more information please refer to the relevant topic introduction pages.

Table 3.1 Topics by season and writing outcome

Topic	*Writing outcome*	*Seasonal suitability*
1 Enchanted forest	Story about two children in an enchanted forest	Spring, summer, autumn
2 Forest club	Story about four children playing in the woods	Spring, summer, autumn
3 Island quest	Diary account of an adventure	Spring, summer, autumn
4 Forest detectives	Crime report	All year round
5 Celtic life	Non-chronological report about life in Celtic times	Spring, summer, autumn
6 Animal world	Non-chronological report about native animals	All year round

What is a session?

A session is a teaching unit for the topic, and each topic has five sessions. Allow forty-five minutes to one hour for each session, and what time you can for the follow-up activity in the classroom afterwards.

Each session will require the preparation of resources, both those listed for the teacher to source and those provided in the appendices for copying. The resources in the appendices have been designed to reproduce clearly on a photocopier, but can be used as the basis for creating something more colourful or visually exciting.

Session structure and rationale

Each of the sessions follows the same structure of: introduction, main activity, review, follow-up activity. The purpose and rationale for this structure are explained below.

Introduction

For the first session of a new topic, the purpose of the introduction is to present your class with a way in to the topic, via letter, coded message or strange occurrence. For all subsequent sessions, the purpose of the introduction is twofold: to recap the class's adventures so far and to introduce the next activity.

The recap is important because it allows children who were absent from the last session to update themselves on developments, but it also gives their classmates a chance to place the upcoming activity within the context of an ongoing narrative. This primes them to make a link between their previous learning experiences, as being discussed by their teacher and peers, and the learning experience that they are about to engage in. It also helps them to rehearse the narrative arc of their experiences, which will be particularly helpful for children who need support with sequencing events and giving reasons for what happened and why.

Tips for the introduction

To ensure that the discussion is not dominated by the ideas of a few children or the instructions of the teacher, ask the children to discuss questions such as those given below in pairs (also known as 'talk partners') before sharing them with the wider class:

- How did our adventure start?
- What have we done so far?
- What did we do last session/last week/yesterday?
- What might have happened since?
- What do you think might happen today/what do you think we might be asked to help with today?

Open questioning and talk partners

Once the latest activity is known to the class, check for understanding by inviting contributions on how to go about it. For example, if the class have received a letter asking for help with hiding food from bears, give the class a moment to discuss in talk partners before inviting comments to the wider class. If it's clear that no one really has any ideas, suggest one yourself – *well, I wonder if digging a hole would work?* – and draw out their responses, e.g. *I see, so a hole would only work if I covered it up . . . what could I use for that?* The purpose of this elicitation activity is to broaden the 'ideas horizon' of the children by exposing them to a wider range of ideas before setting out. In part, this provides them with some ideas to borrow if they are stuck, but it also underscores the fact that there are a range of possibilities.

Main activity

This will be designed to increase the children's experience and understanding within the topic, and will be highly practical, kinaesthetic and physical. The main activity will take a range of forms, such as creating things, playing games or using drama to explore an idea.

Tips for the main activity

I know that this is stating the obvious, but: read the session plan beforehand, prepare the resources and activity area, and brief your teaching assistant.

Some activities involve recording ideas. To ensure that your reluctant writers contribute to the activity and remain engaged, pair or group them with a willing writer who can act as a scribe while they articulate their thoughts out loud. All sessions include plenty of discussion of ideas in pairs, groups or whole class. Actively include the quieter children by priming their contribution, e.g. *Jordan noticed something really interesting when he was making the roof for his shelter. Could you tell the rest of the class what it was?* Encourage their contributions early in any discussion so that the 'safer' comments that they know are correct have not yet been given.

Review

Like a plenary, the review can be as brief or as extended as you wish. Unlike a plenary, the focus is not to underline a teaching point or extend understanding of it. Rather, it is a space for the children to reflect on what they have done during the session and then articulate those thoughts to their peers.

Bearing in mind that your class will be spread out across a site and will have worked in various groupings during the session, one of the easiest ways to hold this review is in two steps.

Session review process

Step 1: Use an agreed signal to indicate that your class should stop their work and discuss what they have done today in their groups or pairs. Direct their discussion by asking questions such as:

> *Has anything surprised you today? What was your favourite bit of the session? What have you learned that you didn't already know? Can you think of ways in which you and your friend(s) worked well together today? Did you find out something interesting today?*

Allow up to five minutes.

Step 2: If the children have created something, such as a hiding place or sculpture, lead the children on a tour around the site. As you pass each piece of work, the children who created it step out and explain what they have made to their peers. You may want to facilitate questions or positive feedback from the rest of your class. Allow five to ten minutes for this.

Follow-up activity

The follow-up activity takes place in the classroom and comes in two parts. It can take as few or as many minutes as you can spare! Being realistic, you won't always have time for all the activities, but the key thing is for your class to have completed the first part, which is normally feeding back their findings to the story characters and updating the woodland wall (although you or a teaching assistant will complete this task).

The second part is designed to let the class discuss the topic in a wider sense, perhaps creating a word bank or exploring ideas in small groups. Suggestions for both parts of the follow-up activity will be given on each session plan.

Updating the woodland wall

After the session has finished, update the woodland wall in your classroom with any (or all!) of the following:

- a copy of this session's letter, email or coded message
- photos of your class taken during the session
- copies of letters, pictures or maps prepared by your class (or findings that they record after the session if there are none)
- word bank relating to the topic, compiled through class discussion
- items brought in from home by the children that relate to the topic.

The purpose of the woodland wall is threefold. Firstly, it serves as an *aide-mémoire* to help the children recall their exploits during the recap for the next session, and also helps out children who have missed part of the topic through illness or other absence. Secondly, it makes the transfer of the children's outdoor experience into the classroom explicit by providing a link between both learning environments. And thirdly, it provides a way of boosting the confidence of children whom you wish to reframe as 'writers' by displaying their follow-up work. Seeing that their map or annotated picture has equal validity to an able child's lengthy account will be very powerful. It goes without saying that the work displayed on this board might not be the neatest, but to demand neatness would be to miss the point. It's not meant to be a celebration of tidy presentation, but evidence of the spontaneous recording that the children can produce when inspired.

Modifying the session content – or creating your own topic

The activities within each topic have been chosen to build up the children's first-hand experience and understanding over the duration of the topic, so that they can draw upon these when producing the writing at the end. At some point, you are bound to find that you need to tailor the activities suggested to fit the time, resource or ability constraints within your class. You may choose to eschew the 'Simplify/Extend' guidance for something better suited to your class and setting. You may even decide to create your own writing topic.

When doing so, bear in mind the importance of providing a first-hand experience that will increase the children's knowledge of the topic. The checklist below will help to ensure that the replacement activity is true to the spirit and intention of the original.

Problem-solving role

Have you placed the main activity in a problem-solving context? How will the class be encouraged to verbalise and share their ideas? How will group size affect this (positively or negatively) and does it need to be set?

Kinaesthetic and collaborative

What will the children actually get to do, make, build or test out today? What opportunities are there for them to discuss their ideas and work with their peers?

Actors in the story

How will the children's activities be central to the progress of the story, and how will the narrative device be used to introduce the session content?

Recap and review

What opportunities will there be for the children to recap the story so far and their actions within it, and to reflect on their efforts that day?

Embedded final writing outcome

If creating a new topic, how will you present the writing task within context and not as an isolated classroom task?

Topic theme

If creating a new topic, what theme is going to link your sessions into a coherent whole?

Narrative device

Which device will be most suitable or exciting? Letters, coded messages, emails, voice recordings that the children don't recognise (perhaps you can enlist the help of your offspring or spouse . . .)?

Suspending disbelief, and dealing with questions

Each of these topics relies upon the teacher going along with the story theme, however implausible it might seem to adult ears. A willingness to seem 'swept along' with the rest of your class is essential, because some children will decide how to respond by watching you. After all, it's not every day that a letter turns up on the windowsill from two children lost in an enchanted forest, and the less credulous in your class will want to know whether you are going to dismiss it or give it some consideration.

You don't need to put on an Oscar-winning performance. A puzzled frown upon discovery of the letter, a preface of 'well, this is rather strange but . . .' before reading it out will indicate enough interest on your part without having to lie outright about whether it's true.

If your class ask if it's true, 'I don't know' is a reasonable answer. But a better answer is, 'Well I don't know. What do you think?' turning the burden of analysis back onto them. Facilitate their discussion and indicate that you are keeping an open mind. This is where a few props, such as a bird's feather dropped on the windowsill next to the delivered letter, pay huge dividends, as they provide possible evidence and give the children licence to get swept away with the story. See the 'Wow factor' on session plans for further prop ideas.

Investing in the story

You can probably see by now that the more effort you put into creating an atmosphere of excitement and possibility – whether through finding special props at home, following some of the Wow-factor suggestions or improving upon the resources in the appendices of this book – the better. This won't come as a surprise; you're a teacher! Just like any other scheme of work, the more consideration you put into how it will work for your class, the better you will engage them, the deeper their learning experience will be, the stronger the bond will be between you all from a shared adventure, and the more enthusiasm for the next session.

Embedding the final writing outcome in the topic

One of the educational theories that has inspired me over the years is Dorothy Heathcote's 'mantle of the expert'. In a nutshell, 'mantle of the expert' is a creative model of teaching and learning that encourages children to imagine themselves in real-life dilemmas faced by experts in wide-ranging fields and, through drama, to explore and implement solutions to them. An example would be setting up a museum in your classroom that specialised in the Romans, only to find that all the exhibits that were to be delivered had been destroyed in a warehouse fire. The children, in their role as museum workers, would decide how to replace them, make the artefacts for display, discuss how to advertise the museum to the wider school community and produce publicity materials, write programmes to explain the exhibits and maybe even make and sell refreshments. This model of teaching and learning includes plenty of opportunities for purposeful writing, and all of them embedded within the topic.

Placing the writing outcome within the context of the topic makes the link explicit, capitalising on the sense of expertise that the children have built up through first-hand experience. Some will view it as a favour to the topic characters or an investigation on their behalf, leading to higher levels of motivation than might typically be seen for writing. It's writing, yes, but it's different; there is a heightened sense of purpose, the child's internal picture of the audience might be different (e.g. story characters rather than teachers), and the child's sense of being equal to the task is increased through their first-hand experience, which they can draw upon. In the words of Crumpler (2005), an experienced practitioner of drama-based learning:

> If writing is viewed as a separate, more serious activity that children complete after the drama is over rather than as a feature of the . . . work, the imaginative energy created from moving back and forth from the real to the fictional is diluted, and possibly lost altogether.
>
> (p. 359)

Practical tips to link the writing task to the topic

If at all possible, take the children to the site to write, using clipboards (or, failing that, whiteboards with paperclips to hold the sheet on). The children can spread out, finding somewhere comfortable, quiet and inspiring. Separate children who you know will find it hard to settle, and provide a tarp to sit on if you think it's 'damp bottom' weather.

Before starting to write, encourage the children to notice and absorb the atmosphere – move through the senses of what they can see, hear, smell and feel. Bring out any supplies required – pencils, rubbers, sharpeners, spare paper – and move around the group, quietly dispensing and collecting. I am always astonished by how effective this technique is. If the work ends up a bit messy, this can be treated as a first draft that will be marked, written in best and then made into a class book.

If writing outside is not possible, some tips for concluding the topic indoors are given below.

- Draw the children's attention to the woodland wall and features that might be relevant, such as word banks or photos of activities. Use talk partners to let the children rehearse their ideas with their peers before they start to write. If artefacts are to hand, put them out on the tables for children to look at when stuck for inspiration.
- You may have a piece of music or an internet sound-clip that you could play in the background as they write, creating a feeling in the classroom that the writing they are engaging in is something above and beyond the ordinary. If you have been using a particular piece of music during the follow-up activity, this would be the obvious choice. Otherwise, choose something evocative. Avoid anything with a clear vocal in English, as the lyrics will be distracting, although foreign languages can sound beguiling. Equally, avoid anything too strident or dramatic; I once played Prokofiev's 'Dance of the Knights' (now a regular fixture in a reality television programme) to a Year 5 class and it punctured the atmosphere completely, resulting in mass hysteria and a peevish teacher.
- Turn some of the lights off to create a secretive atmosphere, or put on a special light such as fairy-lights or a lava lamp from home.
- Create a set of images relevant to the topic on your interactive whiteboard. The children can gaze at this while searching for inspiration. It's best to avoid pictures of your class here, as they might prove too distracting. Instead, do an internet search for themed images, such as animal photos, Celtic artefacts or settings relevant to the topic story. See 'ICT skills' in Chapter 10 for more details on how to create an image sequence.

4 Topic 1: The enchanted forest

Summary

Help Carrie and Farid, two children who are lost in an enchanted forest, to escape by investigating their problems and advising them on what to do.

Guidance

Narrative device: The children communicate with your class via letters, as delivered by a friendly owl.

Characters: Carrie and Farid.

Activity summary: Building mini-shelters using natural materials, looking into ways to hide food from hungry bears, finding ways to avoid getting lost, creating camouflage using natural materials.

Resources

The basics

- Plenty of natural materials in activity site, such as sticks, twigs, stones, gravel, wood-chippings, leaves, garden clippings, weeds etc.
- Glue, sheets of newspaper, string, scissors, glue sticks, sellotape (several rolls)
- Imitation food (such as plastic toy food found in Reception play corners)
- Materials for laying trails: stones, gravel, leaves, feathers, string, bottle-tops, pegs, coloured paper scraps etc.
- Fifteen plastic or paper cups
- Fifteen plastic coins
- Letters from Carrie and Farid (see appendices)
- Four to six trowels or gardening forks

Wow factor

- Real food to hide, such as a bunch of bananas or red apples (choose something bright)

- A bird's nest to place the letters in (either make one yourself out of some twigs, or check the dusty corners of the stock cupboard for one donated by parents when it fell out of a tree in their garden)
- A couple of natural-coloured feathers to place in your classroom, to indicate that the owl has visited
- A ribbon for rolling up and tying the letters from your class/Carrie and Farid
- When preparing the letter for each session, edit and retype the letter from Carrie and Farid to reflect the experiences of your class

Writing outcome

To write a story about two children having an adventure in an enchanted forest.

Follow-up activities

Communicating findings to Carrie and Farid via letters.

Discussing wider thoughts about activities so as to share ideas with peers and expand vocabulary.

Curricular links

Literacy: story-writing and describing settings

Author's comments

This is a great 'starter topic', as each session requires a minimum of preparation, and will get you and your class used to the rhythm of moving outdoors for learning.

Session 1: Building mini-shelters

Your class will discover a letter from two children lost in an enchanted forest. They will be asked to help them, firstly with building a shelter to sleep in.

Resources

Teacher

- Bird's nest/pile of twigs
- Plenty of natural materials in activity site
- Feathers (one or two, natural in colour)
- Piece of ribbon or string
- Digital camera

Book

- Appendix T1L1 (letter)

Preparation

- Place a real bird's nest, or create one from twigs, on a windowsill or shelf near a window, for the delivery and collection of all letters.
- Roll up this session's letter like a scroll, and tie with the ribbon. Place on top of the nest. (Do this during playtime or lunchtime, so that the class do not see.)
- Check that the activity area has plenty of natural materials for building mini-shelters.
- Gather up any other resources required.

Session plan

1. If the children do not draw your attention to it, suddenly remark upon the bird's nest and letter. Read the letter to the class, inviting comments and ideas to check for understanding.
2. Once in the activity area, sit your class down in a circle/group and invite them to recap what has happened so far: we have received a letter from two children lost in an enchanted forest; they need our help to build a shelter.
3. Advise your class that they will be building 'mini-shelters', which are like models of a full-size shelter. They can work in pairs, small groups or individually (subject to any arrangements you have made with individual children/your teaching assistant). They can build their mini-shelters anywhere within the activity area. Elicit ideas to check for understanding again if you think it appropriate (for example: *I wonder what they would use for the roof? Do you think they would need a light? What could you do with soft leaves like this? Does anyone think that an acorn would be useful? How?*)

4. Move around the group as the children build, encouraging them and commenting upon their ideas.
5. Review the activity (see 'Session review process' on pages 26–7 for guidance) and take photos or ask your teaching assistant to do so while you facilitate the discussion.
6. Tidy up and return to the classroom.

Follow-up activity

Step 1: Reply to the children's letter, telling them your ideas for how to build a shelter.

Step 2: Make a word bank of the materials used, with interesting adjectives to describe them, e.g. *dry sticks*, *shiny leaves*, and add to the woodland wall, along with photos from the session's activities.

Tips

ICT: If completing the letter as a shared write, try composing it on your interactive whiteboard so that the children can edit and improve it as you go.

Behaviour management: If this is the first time your class has visited the activity area, they may be very excited and find listening quite a challenge. Agree in advance with them what signals you will use to gain their attention and what behaviours you will expect. If you have a woodland charter, refer to this to remind them of its content.

Simplify: The teacher can facilitate a class discussion that results in a shared write for the letter to Carrie and Farid, telling them about what has been found for building the shelters.

Extend: Ask your class to compose individual letters to the children to report on their findings about how to build shelters. They can use words, pictures, annotated diagrams or a mix of these. Collect in all the letters at the end of the time allotted for the follow-up activity, tie with the ribbon and leave on the nest for collection. (It is important that these letters are treated as being for Carrie and Farid's eyes only, and not intended for marking by the teacher.)

Session 2: Hiding food from the bears

Carrie and Farid thank your class for their assistance and ask for further help, this time with hiding their food supply from the bears.

Resources

Teacher

- A ball of string
- Three or four pairs of scissors
- Plastic or real food to hide
- A few trowels or gardening forks
- Digital camera

Book

- Appendix T1L2 (letter)

Preparation

- Print off the letter and place it on the bird's nest as before.
- Find some plastic imitation food (try the Reception or KS1 classes if you have none) or real food that is brightly coloured, e.g. red apples, bananas, for your class to hide.
- Decide, depending on how much you have, whether you want the children to work in pairs or individually (think about whether you need to avoid specific children working together and plan accordingly).
- Gather up any other resources required.

Session plan

1. Discover the latest letter, and recap what happened during the last session before reading it aloud.
2. Check for understanding from the children about what they have been asked to do before going to the activity area.
3. Before starting the activity, sit in the area and elicit ideas about where they might hide things and what the advantages or disadvantages might be for each place. Hand out the food to be hidden to pairs/groups. Show the children from where to borrow string/scissors/trowels if they decide that they need them and agree rules for returning them after use.

If you have plenty of trees on site, decide in advance how high up the trees you are happy for your class to reach or climb, and communicate this clearly. A rule I often use is 'one step up', meaning that they can step up onto a low branch, but no higher. Whatever you decide, stick well within the limits of your school's health and safety policy and what you are comfortable with.

4. Children work on creating a hiding place for the food. Move around the site, assisting with tying knots and helping children to use the trowels effectively (scoop and dig at a shallow angle). If the children can't cut their own string, have lengths ready or take the ball around with some scissors to groups.
5. Review the session.
6. Collect any equipment and return to class.

Follow-up activity

Step 1: As before, choose whether you respond as a whole class or individually, then bundle up the letters and leave on the nest for collection.

Step 2: Are bears the only kind of animal that you might find in an enchanted forest? Make mind-maps in groups of the other kinds of animals that might live there, and what magical abilities they might have. Update the woodland wall with photos of the session.

Tips

ICT: Use the interactive whiteboard software to create a letter from the class, or a class mind-map of the animals you might find in an enchanted wood. If you have a visualiser or a projector, try putting the letter on it for the whole class to read at the same time.

Behaviour management: Prepare the string and put your teaching assistant with a small group of children who you think might become discouraged if they are not able to tie knots very easily.

Simplify: Younger children will need help with tying knots, and also with cutting string. Cut lengths in advance, or ask your teaching assistant to be on 'string and scissors' duty. They might also need help getting started with digging a hole – help them locate somewhere more suitable by finding looser, soily ground rather than grass.

Extend: Encourage your class to think not just about hiding the food but also about things like decoys, hidden pits, or simple levers which, once pressed by the bear's paw as it walks along, cause a net or similar to fall over its head. Can they incorporate some of these ideas into their design?

Session 3: Trail marking

Help Carrie and Farid avoid getting lost as they move around the forest, by creating a way to mark their trail.

Resources

Teacher

- Different materials to experiment with: gravel, sand, sticks, feathers, leaves, shells, coloured paper scraps, string, bottle tops etc. Anything that you can think of!
- Fifteen paper or plastic cups
- Fifteen plastic coins (silver ones best)
- Scissors
- Digital camera

Book

- Appendix T1L3 (letter)

Preparation

- Gather as wide a range of materials as you can for creating trails (see list above), anticipating that the children will work in pairs.
- Place the materials in containers – such as the plastic cups suggested above – and hide them around the site.
- Print the letter and place on the nest as usual.
- Gather up any other resources required.

Session plan

1. Discover the letter and, before reading, use talk partners to recap what adventures we have had so far with Carrie and Farid. Make use of the woodland wall as appropriate.
2. Read the letter and check for understanding with the children. Find out if anyone has laid trails before at Beavers or Brownies and ask them to explain what they used.
3. Once at the activity area, sit the children in a circle and ask them to look around quietly and see if they notice anything that shouldn't be there. Once someone has noticed one of the containers, explain that there are more hidden, and that they contain materials that they could use for a trail. The children find all the containers and then return them

to the circle. Show the children the contents of each cup. Explain that they will take it in turns to set a trail for their partner in order to find a small piece of treasure.

4. In pairs, the children select a cup and then the teacher splits them into two groups, 1 and 2. The children who are in group 1 hide their treasure and then lay a trail leading to it from the circle. The children in group 2 sit in a row with their backs to their partners so they can't see where they're hiding the treasure, and discuss the following: which of these materials might be best for being seen in the dark; for being camouflaged in the local environment; on a windy day; if it rains hard. When the group 1 children have finished laying their trails, they come and sit behind their partners. Ask your teaching assistant to supervise the children doing the trail laying while you facilitate the discussion.
5. The children in group 2 are shown the beginning of the trail laid by their partner and have to follow it to find the treasure. Once they have done so, they return to sit at the edge of the activity area.
6. Once all the children in group 2 have found their treasure, the groups swap over and repeat the activity.
7. Review: ask the children to reflect in pairs on which types of trail worked well, and which were less useful, as they walk around the activity area looking at the various trails laid out on the ground. The children collect up the materials that need to be taken back inside in the cups and return to the classroom.

Follow-up activity

Step 1: Write a letter to Carrie and Farid to inform them of your findings (shared write or individual).

Step 2: Update the woodland wall with pictures from the session and discuss the materials tested in the session, and which one would work best in an enchanted forest. Can they think of any other things they could have used? Why would these be better?

Tips

ICT: As before, use a visualiser or a projector to share the letter with the class, and the interactive whiteboard to share writing and editing of a letter from the class.

Behaviour management: Make sure that the children understand which group is sitting with you and which is setting trails. Also, explain that the object is to find the piece of treasure hidden by *their* partner, not just the first piece that they come across. If you are concerned about children snatching coins up willy-nilly, add an extra rule that the child hunting the treasure must check with their partner that they have found the right one before picking up the coin.

Simplify: For very young classes, you could put a big pile of 'treasure' on the ground and then, from the edge of the activity area, they can work in pairs to make a trail that leads to it. They can choose to make their trail lead straight to it, or weave around features such as bushes or trees.

Extend: Can the children find cunning places to hide their treasure, such as under stones, up trees, in holes? Can they think of ways to communicate instructions in their trail, such as *left*, *right*, *look above*? Ask them to include this information in their letter afterwards.

Session 4: Making camouflage hats

Create a camouflage hat to wear while climbing up the side of the Misty Mountain, thus evading the attention of the dragons.

Resources

Teacher

- Thirty sheets of newspaper
- Five rolls of sellotape
- Five pairs of scissors
- Ten glue sticks
- Plenty of natural materials such as leaves, twigs, flowers, moss etc.
- Digital camera

Book

- Appendix T1L4 (letter)

Preparation

- Prepare the letter and place it on the nest.
- If your class is younger, you will need to fold the newspaper sheets into a simple hat in advance. See Chapter 10 for more details.
- Ensure that the activity area is full of natural materials that can be attached to the newspaper hats, such as twigs, leaves, weeds, husks, grass clippings etc.
- Gather up any other resources required.

Session plan

1. Discover the latest letter. As ever, recap the story so far using talk partners, before reading the latest message.
2. Check for understanding about the task that has been set, and what the word 'camouflage' means. Can anyone think of times when it is used?
3. Go out to the activity area. Briefly show the children the materials that have been provided for cutting and sticking, and agree appropriate rules to ensure sharing.
4. If your class are folding their own newspaper sheets, get them all to sit in a circle and copy you, one step at a time. If your class is getting straight on with sticking, send them off to start collecting materials to add to their hats.
5. Move around the site, helping children who are stuck. Encourage those finishing early

to cover the entire surface of their hat, or to help out other children who are taking longer.

6. Once the children have finished, get them all to wear their hats and hide. Take a photo from the edge of the activity area to add to your woodland wall or use on the interactive whiteboard later (see below).
7. Review: children find a partner and take it in turns to tell each other what they used to make their hats. Then they find a new partner and repeat this (this will be easier than trying to facilitate a tour of 30 different heads!).
8. Tidy up and return to the classroom.

Follow-up activity

Step 1: Complete a letter to update Carrie and Farid about what was discovered.

Step 2: Update the woodland wall with pictures from the session and some examples of the camouflage hats. Look at the picture you took of the class hiding in their hats on the interactive whiteboard, or put an A4 size print on your woodland wall. Whom can you spot?

Tips

ICT: Upload the photo that you took of your class hiding with their camouflage hats on to your computer. View it as a whole class on the interactive whiteboard, trying to spot as many children as possible.

Behaviour management: The quantities of sellotape and glue may seem excessive, but it's better to avoid children becoming frustrated because they can't get on with their work. Be prepared to sacrifice a couple of glue sticks to the gods of outdoor learning when they become completely encrusted with soil and bits of twigs!

Simplify: Be prepared for plenty of demands for help, and enlist another adult to help or allow extra time. Alternatively, make a few piles of materials that the children can help themselves to, so that they don't spend so much time roaming around the activity area and are closer by to assist. They could also work in pairs to create a camouflage hat.

Extend: Encourage your class to cover the entirety of their hats, leaving no gaps.

Session 5: Writing stories to read in the cave

The children are waiting for the Wizard to cast a spell that will send them home. While they wait in their cave, they would like some exciting stories to read.

Resources

Teacher

- Paper and writing materials for the children to write their stories
- Clipboards or whiteboards with paperclips for holding the sheet in place
- Woodland wall and artefacts created by the children
- Selection of topic photos on interactive whiteboard (if indoors)
- Two sheets of sugar paper, marker pens and Blu-Tack
- Digital camera

Book

- Appendix T1L5 (letter)

Preparation

- Prepare the letter and place it on the bird's nest.
- Gather up any other resources required.

Session plan

1. Discover the final letter, and ask the children to think up mimes to convey the adventures shared by Carrie and Farid so far before reading the message.
2. Read the letter and ask the children what ideas they might use for their adventure story. In talk partners, children think of exciting problems that the characters of their story might face. Be explicit in encouraging the children to draw upon their experiences during the topic. Invite contributions and make a mind-map on the board of their ideas (if you are doing this outside, you can make a mind-map on a large piece of sugar paper and then fasten it to a tree or wall with Blu-Tack).
3. Draw the children's attention to the setting for the story: an enchanted forest. What words and phrases will they use to convey the atmosphere? How will they describe what it looks like? Use talk partners again for the children to explore their ideas. You can make a word bank for them to use, if this is appropriate. Use a sugar-paper sheet to do this if your class are writing outdoors.

4. The children write their stories. Move around the group ensuring that the children have what they need to be able to concentrate. Move children or sit them with the teaching assistant, as appropriate.
5. Send a group of early finishers back to the classroom with the teaching assistant.
6. Once all the children are finished, tidy up and return to the classroom.

Follow-up activity

Step 1: Let the children read each other their stories and give each other feedback on which aspects would appeal to Carrie and Farid.

Step 2: Update the woodland wall with some copies of the stories and photos from the final session.

Tips

ICT: If writing the stories indoors, show a selection of images on the interactive whiteboard that are related to the story theme, while the children are writing, so that they can look at it for inspiration.

Behaviour management: If your class are writing outside, make sure you've got all the kit you need before setting out. Use a tarp to sit on if the ground is quite damp, and make sure all of your class are wearing coats and/or jumpers to avoid too many trips back to the school building.

Simplify: Children can complete a storyboard first, drawing a picture for 'once upon a time . . .', 'then . . .', and 'finally . . .'. They then write simple sentences underneath to explain what is happening at each stage.

Extend: Draw the children's attention to whatever your Literacy focus is, such as expressive punctuation or connectives. Encourage them to use these features too in their stories, to make them even more enjoyable for Carrie and Farid to read.

5 Topic 2: Forest club

Summary

Follow the adventures of four children whiling away the school holidays in the woods, joining in with their games and discoveries.

Guidance

Narrative device: A story told in chapters. This topic is not designed to allow your class to interact with the characters.

Characters: Josh, Shannon, Finn and Farzana.

Activity summary: Making nests, finding things and 'rethinking' them, making puddle-boats, word games, tree collages, story sticks.

Resources

The basics

- Plenty of natural materials, especially sticks, twigs and leaves
- If you are short on twigs for Session 2, provide cocktail sticks or kebab sticks, both available from supermarkets
- Wool or fabric scraps, coloured feathers and foil to decorate the nests
- Paper for tree collages
- Glue sticks
- Sellotape
- Long sticks (enough for one each – about as long as your forearm)
- String
- Sugar paper and marker pens
- A very basic, life-sized shelter built from natural materials
- Clipboards

Wow factor

- A real nest, if you have one stored somewhere, or one that you have made yourself
- A puddle-boat to show the children (see Session 2)
- A tree collage (see Session 3)
- A story stick (see Session 4)
- An authentic 'scene of disturbance' in the activity area (see Session 5)

Writing outcome

A story based on the mysterious scene that the children find in the woods.

Follow-up activities

These will focus primarily on building up descriptive vocabulary for the woodland setting, and also on creating a bank of ideas about possible story scenarios in the same setting.

Curricular links

Literacy/fiction/stories with familiar settings

Author's comments

This is another good topic to start with, as it is very straightforward to prepare and run; it unfolds as a series of short chapters and has no interaction between your class and the story characters built in. This will give you more time to spend on the follow-up activities that will develop your class's ideas for the writing outcome.

It is highly recommended that you prepare examples of the items made by the story characters for each session, especially if this is the first topic you have done outside with your class. This will make it much easier for your class to see what they need to do. This topic works best in spring, summer or autumn.

Session 1: The best of the nests

Find out what Forest Club is and build your own nest.

Resources

Teacher

- Plenty of natural materials in the activity area, especially twigs, sticks, long grass, pine needles etc.
- Any extra materials for decorating the nests, such as foil, feathers, fabric scraps or wool scraps
- A nest, either made or acquired!
- Digital camera

Book

- Appendix T2C1 (first chapter)

Preparation

- Photocopy and roll up the story chapter. Tie with string.
- Hide it in the activity area.
- Gather together any other materials needed, including the nest (or make it on site and leave it there).

Session plan

1. Ask the children if they have ever heard the story of Forest Club. Tell them that you know the story and you can tell them, but they will have to come outside with you to find the first chapter.
2. Let the children find the first chapter of the story, and then seat them in the activity area and read it aloud. Check for understanding. If you have a nest, show it to the children at this point so they can discuss how it has been made. Have they seen any others that look different? E.g. storks' nests.
3. Talk briefly about the requirements for their nests: do they need to be strong? Light? Comfy? Camouflaged? Warm? Tell the children that they will now gather materials in their heads, and then share them with a friend. Put the children in pairs. Without touching anything or talking, the first person in each pair will walk around the activity area, looking for things to use to build their nest and gather them in their head. On your signal, they then return to their partner and tell them what they saw. Swap.

4. Children build nests around the activity area. Encourage them to use a range of materials, sizes, techniques and locations. Show them the materials you have brought outside for decorating the nests. Let them work individually or in pairs.
5. Suggest to early finishers that they could find something precious or special to put in the nest so that it is kept safe.
6. Two-step review process: firstly, the children will evaluate what they have made with their partners (or with another person working alone if they do not have one). Then they will do a tour around the site, stepping out to show the rest of the class their work. Use your questioning to draw the other children's attention to interesting details or techniques.
7. Tidy up and return to the classroom.

Follow-up activity

Step 1: Update the woodland wall with pictures of the nests, or even a real 'nest' made by a child, if this is practical.

Step 2: In small groups of 3-4, without using paper or pencils, the children make up a story about some children who are playing in a wood and find a nest. Whose is it? What is inside? What do they do? What happens next? Listen in as they discuss, and then select a couple of groups to tell their stories to the class.

Tips

ICT: Although reading the story outside is more atmospheric, you could show the story on the interactive whiteboard and read it together, either by typing it into your word processor or scanning it. Use digital photos of the activity to add to the woodland wall.

Behaviour management: If you are concerned about the children charging about the activity area, take them outside, seat them in the activity area and then produce the first chapter from your pocket. As they get used to coming outside, you can hide it for them to find. As ever, be clear in your instructions as to what behaviours are acceptable in and around the activity area.

Simplify: Put the children in pairs to make the nests, and suggest that they all make them at ground level to prevent them from coming apart so easily/falling off a branch.

Extend: Can the children build their nest using just one hand – as if it were a beak? (This will be quite tricky, so let them swap back to two hands when they tire of it!)

Session 2: Rethinking the puddle-boat

Try out Farzana's 'rethinking' game and make your own puddle-boat out of twigs and leaves (see Appendix T2C2).

Resources

Teacher

- Good supply of leaves of many sizes/colours
- Good supply of twigs
- Cocktail sticks/kebab sticks if twigs are in short supply
- Your own puddle-boat (see below)
- Digital camera

Book

- Appendix T2C2 (chapter 2)

Preparation

- Make a copy of the chapter and hide it in the activity area.
- Make a puddle-boat out of two leaves and a twig/cocktail stick by placing one leaf flat as the 'boat', then threading the twig through two holes in the other leaf for the 'sail'. Push the twig 'mast' through the boat to secure it. Leave it somewhere safe in the activity area.
- Gather together any other materials you will need.

Session plan

1. Ask the children what they can remember about Forest Club. Where does it happen? Who goes there? Why? What sort of things do they do? Tell them that there is another chapter ready for them to listen to, and take them outside.
2. Let the children look for the next chapter. Sit them down and then read it aloud. Check for understanding.
3. Tell them that they are going to play the 'rethinking' game. Show them something that you have found, such as a leaf. Ask them in pairs to rethink it. Take their suggestions (try to get at least two different ideas, to reinforce the notion that you can think of as many different uses as possible). For example, a rug for a spider's house, a blanket for a mouse.
4. In pairs, the children walk around the site, taking it in turns to stop, show each other something and 'rethink' it. Sit the children in a circle and ask for volunteers to show

something that they found and 'rethought'. Invite further contributions from the other children.

5. Show the children the puddle-boat that you made, and ask them if they can work out what it is (if you have a puddle nearby to try to sail it across, so much the better!). Briefly tell the children how you made it, but stress that they can make one their way – theirs might look very different, as it would be used for a different animal or will be made from different leaves.
6. Let the children make puddle-boats. If you are using cocktail sticks/kebab sticks, warn the children about the pointed ends before distributing.
7. If you have a pond or large puddle nearby, let the children try to 'sail' their puddle-boats so they can modify their designs (if they are doing this on a pond, you will need to provide adult supervision).
8. Review process: children make and swap partners three times, looking at each other's designs and telling each other how they made their puddle-boats and whom they are for.
9. Tidy up and return to the classroom.

Follow-up activity

Step 1: Update the woodland wall with pictures of the children making their puddle-boats, and one or two puddle-boats if possible.

Step 2: How could you rethink some ordinary things found in the woods to make an exciting story? Ask the children in pairs to rethink a twig, a stone with a hole in it, and a green acorn. Share ideas with the rest of the class.

Tips

ICT: Although reading the story outside is more atmospheric, you could show the story on the interactive whiteboard and read it together, either by typing it into your word processor or scanning it. Use digital photos of the activity to add to the woodland wall.

Behaviour management: Ensure adult supervision for any children testing out their puddle-boats on a pond. Also make sure you're happy that children are using the cocktail sticks/kebab sticks appropriately.

Simplify: Give the children longer to make their puddle-boats, and let them work in pairs. If making holes in the leaves is too hard, provide small blobs of Plasticine for fixing the mast.

Extend: What else can the children create that would be useful for a shrew, using just twigs and leaves? Encourage the children to prototype their ideas.

Session 3: Tree collages

Find lots of different ways of describing a tree, and make your own collage of one.

Resources

Teacher

- A sheet of sugar paper with 'words to describe trees' written at the top
- A list of adjectives, written in large felt-tip letters or printed in a large font size, which could be used to describe a tree
- Blu-Tack
- Sheets of paper for making a tree collage – enough for one per child
- Fifteen glue sticks
- Five rolls of sellotape
- Five pairs of scissors
- Your own tree collage, completed or just started
- Digital camera

Book

- Appendix T2C3 (third chapter)
- Appendix T2L1 (tree adjectives)

Preparation

- Photocopy the latest chapter, roll it up and place it in the activity area.
- Prepare and cut up your list of words, so that they are all separate. Think of as many as you can; ideally each child will have one. See Appendix T2L1 if you need inspiration!
- Create your own tree collage, or at least start one off so that the children can see what you're talking about.
- Gather any other resources required.

Session plan

1. Tell the children that there is another chapter of the Forest Club story waiting for them in the activity area. Before leaving the classroom, recap with them what has happened so far to the children in the story.
2. Once the children have found the latest chapter, sit them down and read it aloud. Check for understanding.

3. If the ground is not too damp, ask them all to lie down on their backs, so that they can look up at the tree-tops. (Even if you have just one fairly large one, they can lie next to each other in a ring, with heads in the middle and feet pointing outwards – you should be able to fit most of them in like this!) Let them take a good look at the tree and raise their hand if they have a word or phrase to describe it.
4. Stick the sugar paper up on a tree/wall with Blu-Tack and explain that we are going to play a quick describing game. Hand out a word to each child. Let them help each other read them, and be on hand to help explain their meanings. Ask the children to look at their word, and think about whether it could describe a tree. If they think it does, they can come up and Blu-Tack it to the sugar paper, reading the word aloud to the rest of the class as they do so. If there are any words left at the end, look at them and discuss as a class whether there are any circumstances when they could be used, e.g. *orange* in autumn.
5. Explain that the children will shortly be making their own tree collage. If you have a large site with plenty of trees, give the children a minute to wander round it quietly, looking for the tree that they want to make a collage of.
6. Quickly model how to stick materials onto the page, and show them your example. Be explicit about the fact that trees come in so many shapes, colours and sizes that the children's collages are bound to look very different from yours. Then start making collages. Sit the teaching assistant with a small group of children who are likely to become distracted quickly, to ensure that they get started. Encourage children to carefully tear larger leaves to get the shape that they want for their tree.
7. As the children finish, create a woodland gallery of their work by asking them to find somewhere to Blu-Tack their collage. Once everyone has finished, let the children walk carefully around the woodland gallery, looking at each other's work. Then sit down in a circle and invite comments from the children about what techniques they used that they were proud of, and which collages they particularly liked and why.
8. Tidy up and return to the classroom.

Follow-up activity

Step 1: Update the woodland wall with photos of the children working and viewing the gallery, and a few examples of the collages by children who don't usually get their work displayed.

Step 2: In groups think about what you could see if you climbed to the top of a tall tree. Make up a simple story about that, and then tell the rest of the class.

Tips

ICT: Although reading the story outside is more atmospheric, you could show the story on the interactive whiteboard and read it together, either by typing it into your word processor or scanning it. Use digital photos of the activity to add to the woodland wall.

Behaviour management: Make sure that you have plenty of glue sticks! Bring out some sellotape too, for good measure. You or your teaching assistant may need to be on 'sellotape duty', cutting lengths and sticking them to a nominated tree trunk or stone for the children to come and collect as they require.

Simplify: Prepare ten words, and discuss them all together before agreeing whether they can be used to describe a tree. Let children work in pairs on their collage, and give them a very simple tree outline on the paper to use. If working on the ground outside is too tricky, try collecting the materials and then doing the sticking indoors on flat desks.

Extend: Include some adjectives that provoke discussion, such as *irritable, confused, yellow.* Invite comments on whether these words could sometimes be used. When making the tree collages, encourage older or more able children to reproduce the shape and dimensions of the tree to make it look as much like a real tree as possible.

Session 4: Story sticks

Listen to Farzana and Shannon's adventure story and then create your own using a story stick.

Resources

Teacher

- Plenty of sticks! Forearm-length is fine, and you'll need one for each child
- Flowers and leaves are great for this; if you're doing this in late autumn, bring out some feathers, beads and bottle-tops for the class to use instead
- Sellotape (at least eight rolls)
- Large ball of string/wool
- Four to six pairs of scissors (more for older classes)
- Digital camera

Book

- Appendix T2C4 (fourth chapter)

Preparation

- Photocopy, roll up, tie and hide the latest chapter.
- Ensure that you have a stick supply in the activity area.
- Cut lots of pieces of sellotape and place them on a 'sellotape tree' for the children to use.
- Cut several lengths of string and leave the ball and scissors in a nominated place.
- Make a simple story stick for yourself by attaching three or four interesting things to a stick and quickly make up a story in your head that you can tell with it.
- Gather up any other materials required.

Session plan

1. Tell the children that the latest chapter of the Forest Club story is ready for reading. Before leaving for the activity area, ask the children to recap, in order of events, what has happened in the story so far.
2. Once the children have found the latest chapter, read it aloud as they sit listening. Check for understanding.

3. Show the children your story stick, telling them what each object is, and describing it in a way that stimulates their imagination, e.g. *this leaf is really soft, and green, almost the same colour as an emerald.* Before you tell them *your* story, let them discuss in pairs what sort of story they would make up from the objects on your story stick.
4. Tell them your story, with as much dramatic embellishment as you are comfortable with; then show them the materials for making their story sticks. Set any rules about using scissors/string/sellotape, or any limits on the things they can collect. The children can choose whether to make the story stick straight away or think of their story first, but they might find it easier to do both together, finding something interesting and seeing what it makes them think of. Encourage them to regularly retell their 'story so far' to a friend, to help them think of what might happen next.
5. Once the children have finished making their story sticks, let them find a partner and take it in turns to tell their story. Then ask them to swap and do this again. Try to ensure that the children work with two others whose ideas they don't normally hear, either by selecting boy/girl pairs or asking them to work with someone they haven't yet spoken to outside.
6. Tidy up and return to the classroom.

Follow-up activity

Step 1: Update the woodland wall with photos of the activity and some story sticks.

Step 2: Let the children borrow each other's story sticks, and make up a completely different story for the person who made the stick.

Tips

ICT: Although reading the story outside is more atmospheric, you could show the story on the interactive whiteboard and read it together, either by typing it into your word processor or scanning it. Use digital photos of the activity to add to the woodland wall.

Behaviour management: Pair up any children who you think will become distracted very easily with yourself and/or the teaching assistant. Elicit their story before they collect the items, so that they are clear of the narrative in their heads. As in the previous session, designate a 'sellotape tree'. Cut and stick endless pieces to the bark so that children who can't peel and cut the sellotape independently can come and help themselves.

Simplify: Children can work in pairs on their story sticks, helping each other to think of a story first and then finding some objects to attach to the stick that will help them to remember it.

Extend: Show the children how to tie things to their story sticks, and encourage them to try this. It will take more patience and slow them down a bit, but will also let them practise a new skill.

Session 5: A mysterious event

Listen to the final chapter of the Forest Club story, and help the children explain the mysterious events of the previous night.

Resources

Teacher

- A4 writing paper, clipboards, pencils and rubbers if writing outside
- A rough-and-ready shelter in the activity area (the idea is to recreate the scene described in the story, so don't worry if it collapses!)
- A few odd things to indicate that a person might have been staying there, such as a shoe, a necklace or a food wrapper (try Lost Property or the contents of your school bag!)
- Digital camera

Book

- Appendix T2C5 (final chapter)

Preparation

- Photocopy and roll up the chapter and place it in the activity area.
- Per story, make a basic shelter that a child could sit or lie under in the activity area, and then let part of it collapse.
- Scatter the other items around nearby, so the children can spot them.
- Gather up any other materials required.

Session plan

1. Tell the children that you don't know if the latest chapter is in the activity area, but you think they should go and take a look anyway. Before leaving, let the children recap in pairs what has happened to the four story children so far. Which has been their favourite bit?
2. As you approach the site, tell the children that the caretaker told you that he saw some movement in there yesterday evening. Ask them to let you know if they see anything unusual as they are looking for the story chapter.
3. Don't worry if the children discover the ruined shelter while looking for the latest

chapter – unless your activity area is enormous, this will be impossible to avoid. Let them speculate briefly about what they've discovered before reading the chapter aloud.

4. Explain to the children that they will have to solve the mystery of what happened to the Forest Club area, and then write a story about it. Discuss the ideas of the story children with your class. Can they think of any other scenarios? Draw out their ideas to create a storyline, for example: *So do we think the necklace belongs to the person who was hiding here? Why were they hiding? If the necklace didn't belong to the person, whose was it and why did it end up here?* Put the children in groups of three or four to discuss. If you want, you can use drama here to let them act out possible scenarios.
5. Once the children have had time to explore various storylines, ask them to decide what they are going to write to solve the mystery. In pairs, they can tell each other what they have decided and how their story is going to start.
6. Hand out clipboards, writing materials etc. and let the children seat themselves somewhere comfortable to write. Move around offering encouragement. Put your teaching assistant with two or three children who will need constant encouragement to keep writing, and make sure that you pop over regularly to read and praise their efforts.
7. Once enough children have finished, send an early-returning party with the teaching assistant back to the classroom, or go yourself and leave the others with the teaching assistant.

Follow-up activity

Step 1: Update the woodland wall with stories and pictures from outside.

Step 2: Let the children read each other their stories.

Tips

ICT: If you are returning to the class to write, take plenty of pictures of the 'scene' outside so that you can create a set of images for them to glance at when they are taking a break in their writing.

Behaviour management: The children will be terribly excited by the idea that a fugitive of some description was hiding out in their woods! Let them express this by shouting and rushing about looking for other clues; it's always fascinating to see what else they find. If your class seem concerned by the idea of adults being in the activity area at night, steer the discussion towards the idea that maybe it was a child, and remind them that they are speculating about what might have happened in a story.

Simplify: Let the children draw what happened first, before writing a story afterwards.

Extend: Once the children have completed their first draft outside, encourage them to review it and enhance it with descriptive phrases and words to make it even more exciting. They can then 'publish' their work by writing it up in best.

6 Topic 3: Island quest

Summary

Four children who work for an international wildlife charity travel to a remote island to investigate an animal called the moon-beast. Help them to solve practical problems and assess evidence.

Guidance

Narrative device: Email

Characters: Connie, Ty, Joe and Sammy

Activity summary: Building sun-shelters, making rafts, jigsaw search and artist's impressions/preliminary reports, dramatic reconstructions.

Resources

The basics

- Plenty of natural materials, including leaves, sticks, twigs, branches
- String, needles and thread
- Newspaper
- Strips of sacking or hessian, needles and thread (children can sew pieces together and decorate with leaves)
- Empty plastic water bottles with lids (a mix of sizes is fine – try asking the children with packed lunches to give you their empties)
- Water trays or a full sink of water in the classroom

Wow factor

- Exotic leaves and grasses, e.g. prunings from ferns, rubber plants, banana palms etc. (ask around in the staffroom)
- School pond for testing rafts
- Set up two free email addresses for sending and receiving the children's emails; this will also allow you to view

them easily on the interactive whiteboard and compose a response as a class. See 'ICT skills' in Chapter 10 for guidance on how to do this.

Writing outcome

Adventure story (for younger or less able children)
Adventure diary (for older or more able children)

Follow-up activities

Sending an email (as a class or individually) to update the story characters. Compiling a word bank on the woodland wall to describe the characters' emotional responses to events.

Curricular links

ICT: There is potential for extensive use of ICT here as the children communicate with the story characters via email after each session.

Author's comments

For the best results, set up two email accounts – one that 'belongs' to the story characters and to which your class can send their messages, and one for your class, to which the story characters will 'send' their replies. It really adds to the excitement and authenticity of the communication. Guidance on how to set up the email accounts is given in 'ICT skills' in Chapter 10, but you may have an email software package set up for internal use that you could use; ask your ICT co-ordinator.

Sending and receiving emails means that someone will have the job of typing in the latest message from the story characters – you! Depending on your typing speed, set aside an additional 5–10 minutes' preparation time for this before each session.

This story unfolds on a remote tropical island, so the more weird and wonderful the flora you can introduce into the activity area for the children to use, the better. Fern fronds, dead rubber plants, spider plants that have seen better days, bracken and ferns, even coconut shells . . . Whatever you can lay your hands on.

Session 1: Building a sun-shelter

Help Ty, Connie, Joe and Sammy create a shelter to protect them from the heat of the tropical sun.

Resources

Teacher

- Plenty of natural materials, including leaves, sticks, twigs, branches
- String, scissors, needles and embroidery thread
- Exotic leaves and grasses, e.g. prunings, ferns, rubber plants, banana palms etc.
- Strips of sacking or hessian, needles and thread (children can sew pieces together and decorate with leaves)
- Newspapers
- Digital camera

Book

- Appendix T3L1 (introductory email)

Preparation

- If you have set up email addresses, then type up the content of Appendix T3L1 as an email from the four children and send it to the account for your class.
- Log in to your class's email account and make sure the first email from the story characters has arrived.
- If using a paper copy of Appendix T3L1, copy it and place it on your desk.
- Distribute any prunings or cuttings that you have obtained around the activity area.
- Thread some large needles with embroidery thread (this is thicker and easier to see).
- Gather together any other equipment that you will be taking to the activity area.

Session plan

1. Tell the children that you have received a strange email that you would like them to take a look at. Show them the email on the interactive whiteboard and read it together.
2. Use talk partners to allow the children to discuss their reaction to the email; they may have questions about where the island is, why the children have been sent there etc.

Refer them back to the content of the email, but allow them to speculate about the situation. Check for understanding about the task by eliciting ideas about what to do/what to use. Encourage suggestions for how the needle and thread might come in useful.

3. Go to the activity area and seat the children. Explain any things that they are not allowed to use, and model using the needle and thread to sew leaves or other items to the sacking/hessian, if they are using it. Allow the children to work in group sizes of 1–3. For older children, let them start creating a sun-shelter. If you have no sacking, children can use sheets of newspaper to drape over their structures.
4. Move around the site helping children whose needles have become unthreaded or who need scissors or help tying knots. Encourage a range of ways of attaching the materials together by modelling ideas with groups who are stuck, e.g. driving a stick into the ground to support the weight of a covering, or using a grid made of sticks to place things on.
5. Review the activity, first in groups and then by moving around the site to look at each other's ideas (see 'Session review process' on pages 26–7 for guidance on how to do this).
6. On your return to the classroom, compose a reply to the story characters' email and send it, using the interactive whiteboard to make this a shared process.

If you have access to an ICT suite or set of laptops, pair the children up and they can compose and type their own responses, logged on to the class's email account.

Follow-up activity

Step 1: Compose a response to the characters' email and send it to the class email account.

Step 2: Start a word bank on the woodland wall with words to describe how the children must have felt during their first day on the island.

Tips

ICT: Set up the email accounts mentioned earlier. You can then get your class to send emails from the class's account to Sammy, Connie, Ty and Joe and read them together on the interactive whiteboard. If you have taken digital photos of the children's sun-shelters, download them onto a shared drive so that the children can send them as attachments to their emails.

Behaviour management: Thread the children's needles in advance if your class are young or easily distracted. If they are older, leave the needles unthreaded as an additional challenge!

Simplify: If using needles is too tricky for young fingers, you could always have a roll of sellotape up your sleeve. Show the children how to drape some sacking or hessian over structures that already exist, such as low branches, and then cover it with leaves to provide better shade.

Extend: Ask the children to build a life-sized shelter with room for two children to sit under it at one time; this will encourage some more ambitious structural designs. Encourage using a range of fixing techniques, such as knots, stitches, lattices.

Session 2: Building rafts

Help the children to build rafts that will carry them and their supplies to an islet in the middle of a freshwater lagoon.

Resources

Teacher

- Twigs, branches, natural materials
- String and scissors
- Stones
- Empty plastic water bottles with tops (a mix of sizes is fine)
- Water trays/full sink of water in the classroom/school pond
- Digital camera

Book

- Appendix T3L2 (second email)

Preparation

- If you have set up email addresses, then type up the content of Appendix T3L2 as an email from the story characters and send it to the class email account.
- Log in to your class's email account and make sure that the latest email has arrived.
- If using a paper copy of Appendix T3L2, copy it and place it on your desk.
- Gather all materials to be taken to activity area.
- Ensure that there is a good supply of sticks, twigs, branches etc. in the activity area.

Session plan

1. Before reading the latest email, encourage the children to recount the adventure so far. Tell the children that you have received a reply from their new friends that you would like them to take a look at. Show them the email on the interactive whiteboard and read it together.
2. Use talk partners to allow the children to discuss their reaction to the email, and check for understanding with questions such as: *Has anyone travelled on a raft before? What did it look like/what was it made of? How could you use string? Why would an empty bottle be any use?* Ensure that the children understand that they are building mini versions – prototypes – of the rafts to test out their design ideas.

3. Encourage children to work in pairs, so that they can help each other with knots and fastening. Move around the site offering assistance and encouragement.
4. Towards the end of the session, give the children the chance to test their ideas by floating their rafts on water (see suggestions above for where they could do this). Remind them to place a weight on the raft, such as a stone, to imitate the weight of the children.
5. Review the activity in pairs (see 'Session review process', pages 26–7). If possible, let the children look at each other's rafts as they float (or otherwise) on the water.
6. Tidy up and return to the classroom.

If you have access to an ICT suite or set of laptops, pair the children up so they can compose and type their own responses, logged on to the class's email account. Download any photos of their work to a shared drive so that the children can send them as attachments to Connie, Ty, Joe and Sammy.

Follow-up activity

Step 1: Compose a response to the email from Connie and her friends and send it, either individually or as a shared write.

Step 2: Continue the word bank on the woodland wall. Ask your class to think of words to describe their feelings as they worked on their rafts. Choose interesting and expressive ones for addition, such as *frustrated*, *confused*, *concentrating*, *relieved*.

Tips

ICT: Use the interactive whiteboard to read the latest email from Sammy, Connie, Ty and Joe, and compose a response (if doing a shared write).

Behaviour management: Take plenty of string and scissors out, as this will be the main way the children will fix their raft prototypes together.

Simplify: The children could work in small groups, with some finding materials to use and the others trying to fix them together.

Extend: Stress the importance of the raft being able to bear a load. Use weights such as 50g, 100g, 200g etc. to measure the load that their raft will bear.

Session 3: What do we know about the moon-beast?

Help Connie, Ty, Joe and Sammy to make sense of their notes about the mysterious moon-beast.

Resources

Teacher

- Clipboards/whiteboards with paperclips
- Paper, crayons and pencils (younger children)
- Sugar paper and felt tips or whiteboards and whiteboard pens (older children)
- Digital camera

Book

- Appendix T3L3 (third email)
- A set of jigsaws: Appendix T3J1 is for younger children, and Appendices T3J2–T3J5 are for older children

Preparation

- If you have set up email addresses, then type up the content of Appendix T3L3 as an email from the story characters and send it to the class account.
- Log in to your class's email account to make sure that the latest email from the children has arrived.
- If using a paper copy of Appendix T3L3, copy it and place it on your desk.
- Decide which jigsaw set to use and prepare it. If working with a younger or less able class, make four enlarged copies of Appendix T3J1. Mount each one on a different-coloured sheet of card and then cut along the lines to create the jigsaw pieces. If working with older or more able children, make one enlarged copy of each of Appendices T3J2–T3J5. Mount and cut as before.
- Hide the pieces of the jigsaws around the activity area with the coloured-card side facing upwards.
- Gather any other resources required.

Session plan

1. Before reading the latest email, encourage the children to recount the adventure so far. Show the children the latest email from Connie, Ty, Joe and Sammy on the interactive whiteboard. Before leaving the classroom, put the children into four different colour groups, based on the coloured card you used to mount the jigsaws.
2. When you reach the activity area, sit the children down along the edge. Explain that before they can make sense of the notes about the moon-beast, they have got to find

them and put them together. Tell the class that each group has to find a complete set of coloured notes. They will know they have the complete set when they have all the pieces for their jigsaw. Remind the children how to move safely around the site as they search for their pieces in colour groups.

3. Be on hand to help children find any last missing pieces.
4. Once the colour teams have completed their jigsaws, they need to read the information to each other. Younger children will all have the same information, but the older children will all have different information.
5. Encourage younger children to share their ideas of what the moon-beast might look like, based on what they have learned from the jigsaws. Give them paper, with clipboards or whiteboards to lean on, and pencils/crayons to draw with. Encourage them to discuss their ideas with their friends as they draw.
6. Give older children the challenge of turning their jigsaw notes into a paragraph to share with the rest of the class. They can use sugar paper and felt tips, or whiteboards and whiteboard pens for this. If necessary, nominate the scribe for each group, so as to avoid arguments. Once this is completed, the children will then form a circle and each group will present its information in turn to the rest of the class.
7. Tidy up and return to the classroom.

Follow-up activity

Step 1: Compose a reply to the email received at the start of the session, either individually or as a shared write on the interactive whiteboard.

Step 2: Update the woodland wall with words and short phrases to describe the moon-beast and examples of the children's work from outside.

Tips

ICT: As before, use the interactive whiteboard to read the latest email from Sammy, Connie, Ty and Joe, and compose a response if doing a shared write. If you have taken digital photos of the children's work, download them to a shared drive so that the children can send them as attachments to their email.

Behaviour management: If your class are going to turn their jigsaw facts into a paragraph, ensure that you don't have a group of children working together who all dislike writing! Spread any reluctant writers throughout the groups.

Simplify/extend: The differentiated jigsaws provide two levels of complexity for your class. However, if you don't want your class to write their paragraphs outside, you could ask them to complete a mind-map of facts they have learned instead.

Session 4: We think we might have found it!

Try to solve the mystery of what has happened to the children by looking for clues and sending them advice.

Resources

Teacher

- Talking points in activity area
- A few items from Lost Property (see below)
- Digital camera

Book

- Appendix T3L4 (fourth email)

Preparation

- If you have set up email addresses, then type up the content of Appendix T3L4 as an email from the four story characters and send it to the class account.
- Log in to your class's email account and make sure that the latest email from the children has arrived.
- If using a paper copy of Appendix T3L4, copy it and place it on your desk.
- Walk around the activity area and create, or make note of, existing 'talking points' that could indicate the fate of the children. Look for or create the following: scuffed ground, snapped branches or twigs, scraps of fabric to represent clothing caught on tree branches, footsteps, scratches on tree trunks, a discarded child's shoe, clothing or notebook (raid Lost Property for these!). You can then draw the children's attention to them if they do not notice the features themselves.

Session plan

1. Before reading the latest email, encourage the children to recount the adventure so far. Tell the children that you have just read another email from the story characters, but this one is a bit worrying. Read it through on the interactive whiteboard with them, and note how it ends suddenly without them signing off. Use talk partners to discuss what might have happened. Encourage a wide range of speculative answers that use evidence from the adventure so far or from the content of the email.
2. Tell the children that they are going to try to work out what happened to Connie, Ty, Joe and Sammy by imagining themselves in the same situation and looking for clues.
3. Once at the activity area, sit the children down and ask them to think about signs they

could look for that might indicate any of the scenarios they discussed indoors, such as a struggle, having to run away, being kidnapped or dragged off by the moon-beast etc. Supplement their suggestions with other ideas so that they have a range of things to look for, and send them into the area to look for clues.

4. After the children have found some clues, move around the site pointing them out so that the other children can take a look. You will find that the children themselves are very keen to give their theories, so encourage their contributions and don't worry about the noise! Draw their attention to any items or 'talking points' that they may have missed.
5. Sit the children down in a circle and summarise their thoughts and theories about what might have happened to Connie and her friends. Explain that they are going to use a technique called dramatic reconstruction to help them understand what might have happened. Put the children into groups of six and ask them to come up with a short play to show what they think happened.
6. Once the children have practised, watch the plays in the activity area. Use the review to invite constructive comments and ideas about each play.
7. Tidy up and return to the classroom.

Follow-up activity

Step 1: Complete the response to the characters' email, either individually or as a class.

Step 2: Add a selection of 'sound' words to the woodland wall that describe recent dramatic events, such as *snuffling*, *whispering*, *crashing*.

Tips

ICT: As before, use the interactive whiteboard to read the latest email from Sammy, Connie, Ty and Joe, and compose a response (if doing a shared write).

Behaviour management: Some children will find the search for clues outside incredibly exciting and may need reminding about how to move around the site safely. Use what you know about your class to put the children into groups that can work together effectively for the dramatic reconstruction, and limit the amount of time they have to rehearse so they don't get bored and start roaming around the area, disrupting others.

Simplify: If your class are concerned by the mysterious ending of the email, reassure them by reminding them that it's a story, saying that you're sure the children are fine, but isn't it interesting to imagine exciting things that might have happened to them.

Extend: You could ask your class to complete their dramatic reconstruction using only mime, or to concentrate on using dialogue and body language to convey the characters' feelings.

Session 5: Telling our story

Help Connie, Ty, Joe and Sammy write up their adventures for a film.

Resources

Teacher

- Paper and pencils/pens, clipboards if writing outside
- Writing frame as appropriate
- Digital camera

Book

- Appendix T3L5 (last email)

Preparation

- If you have set up email addresses, then type up the content of Appendix T3L5 as an email from the story characters and send it to the class account.
- Log in to your class's email account and make sure that the final email from the children has arrived.
- If using a paper copy of Appendix T3L5, copy it and place it on your desk.
- If you want your class to use writing frames, prepare and copy as appropriate.
- Gather up any other resources required.

Session plan

1. Before showing the children the final email, ask them to recount the story so far. Read the latest email, and give the children time to discuss their responses with their talk partners.
2. Do you agree that the story of Connie and friends is good material for a film? Discuss as a class, and share elements of their adventures that are particularly dramatic or exciting.
3. Before the class start to write their version of the adventure, draw their attention to the woodland wall and the different words on it. Be explicit in noting how the different words could be used, and give the children thirty seconds with their talk partners to come up with uses for some of the words, e.g. *how could you use 'confused' in the context of your adventure story?*
4. The children write up their story. Younger children: write a simple account of their adventures. Older children: write a day-by-day diary account of their adventures.
5. Send a group of early finishers back to the classroom with the teaching assistant. Tidy up and return with the others when finished.

Follow-up activity

Step 1: Send a final email as a class to let the story characters know that you have completed the final task.

Step 2: Let the children read their stories to each other and update the woodland wall with some examples.

Tips

ICT: As usual, use the interactive whiteboard to view the email and compose a shared response.

Behaviour management: If writing outside, allow more time for travelling to and from the activity area and settling down to the task. Capitalise on the atmosphere of being outside by drawing children's attention to the sounds and sensations, such as a breeze or birds calling, that Connie and the others might have noticed on their island.

Simplify: Ask the children to produce a simple account of the adventure, as a story.

Extend: Ask your class to write a diary of events, detailing the adventure day by day.

7 Topic 4: Forest detectives

Summary

Help Perks and Malik, two local detectives, to examine clues, crack codes and prevent crime being committed by some surprising local criminals.

Guidance

Narrative device: A coded message will start each session, which the children will need to crack in order to find the location of the latest message from the detectives.

Characters: Perks and Malik, the two detectives, old Mrs Beattie who cleans the church, the Reverend Grimsby and two local handymen known as Plonk and Snifter.

Activity summary: Decoding confidential reports about suspects, creating artist's impressions of the suspects, examining a crime scene for clues, using a map to find a hidden object, creating a map and marking the location of a hidden object, producing eyewitness accounts of a strange incident.

Resources

The basics

- Some props that might belong to a Reverend and his cleaner, such as: pocket-sized Bible, feather duster or cleaning cloth, glasses, a 'dog collar' made from white card
- A simple, A4-sized map outline of your school grounds
- Simple disguises for two people, such as woolly hats, scarves, coats (see what's languishing in Lost Property)
- Paper, pencils, rubbers, colouring pencils
- A spade or trowel

Wow factor

- A haul of 'treasure' that might conceivably be found in a church, such as embroidered silk cloth, goblets, candlesticks or hand-tooled metal picture frames – use your imagination and some poetic licence!
- One or two 'actors' to play the role of the burglars during a brief incident in the activity area (try adult staff or two obliging Year 6s who can keep a secret)

Writing outcome

A crime report detailing recent events.

Follow-up activities

Writing messages to Perks and Malik to resolve the puzzle set during each session.

Curricular links

Numeracy: map reading and using codes to conceal or reveal information.

Author's comments

This is a classic detective mystery with a twist, so the children are led to believe that two people are responsible for a theft and planning another before being presented with evidence to the contrary.

This topic involves some code breaking using a cipher that some Year 1 pupils will find challenging, but the teacher can do a 'shared solve' with the whole class, or teach the codes to able pupils in advance, placing a 'code breaker' in each group to lead the activity. There are plenty of other activities that the children will enjoy, including making artist's impressions, giving eyewitness accounts and so on. The fourth session relies on the children witnessing a short but crucial 'incident' in the activity area. Two Year 6 children or adults will briefly act out Plonk and Snifter trying to hide the stolen goods and then running off after spotting your class – leaving a bag of booty and some witness statements behind. This scene will take only a minute to act out but will give the children the sense of having truly stepped into the mystery, which they will then be able to solve.

If you want to change the church and Reverend for symbols that better reflect the experiences of your class, ensure that you have edited and retyped the letters in the appendices from the detectives, and also check that information in the coded messages reflects your changes.

Session 1: Find the suspects

Meet detectives Perks and Malik, and help them to identify which of the four suspects wanted for a local robbery might have been on the school grounds.

Resources

Teacher

- Feather duster or cleaning cloth
- White 'dog collar' worn by clergy (make one out of card)
- Pair of glasses
- A small Bible or prayer book
- Four pencils
- Digital camera

Book

- Appendix T4L1 (letter)
- Appendices T4F1–T4F4
- Appendix T4Cipher

Preparation

- Photocopy the first letter (T4L1).
- Make several copies of the code cipher (T4Cipher).
- Photocopy the files on suspects (T4F1–T4F4), roll each one up and tie with string.
- Take the files and letter out to the activity area and place the letter under a tree.
- Hide the rolled up files around the activity area.
- Scatter the cleaning cloth or feather duster, dog collar, glasses and Bible or prayer book around the activity area.
- Write a message backwards on your whiteboard, to tell the children where to find the first letter, e.g. REDNU EHT KAO EERT (under the oak tree).
- Gather up any other resources required.

Session plan

1. Behave as normal, maybe making some announcements to the class or reminding them about homework, while they have time to notice the message on the whiteboard. Once they have drawn your attention to it, feign surprise and demand to know who wrote it and what it means. If they have not already done so, help the children to notice that it seems to be words written backwards, in a code. Decipher it together, and then go to look in the place specified.

2. Seat the children at the edge of the activity area and read the letter aloud, checking for understanding. Let the children go in and look for unusual objects or items and make a pile of what they find (be prepared for them to make some unintended discoveries, like sweet wrappers and deflated footballs – for now, just add them to the pile).
3. Referring to the letter, ask the class what their second job was. Some of them may already have noticed the rolled-up files and brought them out; if there are any missing, let them find those too. Once you have all four of them, put the children into four groups, hand out the ciphers so that they can decode the messages, and pencils for jottings, and let them work on the files.
4. Once all the codes have been cracked, let the children present their findings to the class, one group at a time. Keep track of the four suspects by summarising at the end of each group's presentation, e.g. *So that's three people now, Mrs Beattie the cleaner, the Reverend Grimsby and Ron Plonk. Who's the final suspect?*
5. Ask the children to consider the other evidence that they have found in the activity area and discuss who they think the suspects must be. Invite their comments and ideas, getting them to justify their opinions with reference to the information in the files and the objects found in the activity area.
6. Tidy up and return to the classroom.

Follow-up activity

Step 1: Update the woodland wall with photos of the evidence and decoded files.

Step 2: Ask the children to write a note in reply to Perks and Malik, explaining who they think the two most likely suspects are.

Tips

ICT: Use the interactive whiteboard for writing the coded message, and to produce a shared write to Perks and Malik.

Behaviour management: Some children will be desperate to solve the puzzle and will be likely to shout out their thoughts. Remind your class as often as necessary to put their hands up or wait their turn before sharing their ideas. When putting together the four groups, try to ensure that dominant children who like to take control are spread out evenly.

Simplify: If you have a very young class, you might want to do a 'shared solve' of the suspect files, or have a child in each group who has already been shown how to use the code cipher and can lead their group. You can also write a shared letter to reply to Perks and Malik.

Extend: Ask the children to write their own individual responses to Perks and Malik saying who they think are the most likely suspects (these should be left under the tree for Perks and Malik to collect and so do not need to be marked).

Session 2: What's in the bundle?

Help to make sense of a suspicious bundle found by the main entrance to the church.

Resources

Teacher

- Four copies of a simple, hand-drawn map of the school grounds
- Four 'bundles' containing Appendices T4Cipher, T4Map and T4List, folded up and fastened with an elastic band/paper clip
- Pencils
- Digital camera

Book

- Appendix T4L2 (letter)
- Appendix T4Map
- Appendix T4List
- Appendix T4Cipher

Preparation

- Make a copy of the latest letter (T4L2) and place it under the tree.
- Make four copies of Appendix T4Cipher, Appendix T4Map and Appendix T4List, put one of each together, fold up and fasten with an elastic band or paper clip.
- Hide each of your four bundles around the school grounds and mark the hiding place of each bundle on a separate map (this map should be very quick to prepare, with a rectangle for the school building, circles for prominent trees, a wavy line for any paths, etc.).
- Write a backwards message on the whiteboard, such as: YDAER ROF REHTONA EGNELLAHC?
- Gather up any other resources required.

Session plan

1. Notice the latest message on the whiteboard, and decode it with the children. Before leaving for the activity area, recap on what happened last session: the names of the detectives, what they were investigating, what was found, who the suspects are.
2. Nominate a child to go and look for the message (in the same place as last time). Read it aloud and check for understanding.
3. Keeping the children in the same groups as last time, hand out a map to each group. Give them some time to orient themselves, and then let them go and find their bundle.

They will need a pencil to jot down the words as they decode them. Keep an eye on the groups and ensure that no one child is dominating the discussion.
4. When the information has been decoded, gather the groups together to discuss what they have discovered. Draw the children's attention to the hand-drawn map and ask what they think it shows. Then look at the coded note, and discuss what it says. What do they think they have discovered here? What should they tell Perks and Malik? Discuss in groups.
5. Tidy up and return to the classroom.

Follow-up activity

Step 1: Update the woodland wall with photos and the things found in the 'bundle'.

Step 2: The children write a reply to Perks and Malik, telling them what they think they have found out.

Tips

ICT: Use the interactive whiteboard to write the coded message, and to produce a shared write to Perks and Malik.

Behaviour management: If you were unhappy with the balance in your groups last session, move some children to ensure a better mix that allows more children to contribute. You can also say that two children at a time take it in turns to decode a line of the message, so as to ensure that they all have a try.

Simplify: If you have a very young class, you may want to do a 'shared solve' of the note, or have a child in each group who has already been shown how to use the code cipher and can lead their group. You can also write a shared letter to reply to Perks and Malik.

Extend: Ask the children to write their own individual responses to Perks and Malik. You can also modify the code to make it harder.

Session 3: Wanted!

Use the information available to draw artist's impressions of the new suspects, and create a 'Wanted!' poster.

Resources

Teacher

- 'Wanted!' poster template, thirty copies
- Clipboards
- Pencils, colouring pencils, sharpeners and rubbers
- Blu-Tack
- Two pieces of sugar paper, labelled 'Plonk' and 'Snifter'
- Digital camera

Book

- Appendix T4L3 (letter)
- Appendices T4F5 and T4F6

Preparation

- Photocopy the latest letter and hide it in the usual place.
- Make a copy of Appendices T4F5 and T4F6 and cut up the different bits of information into strips.
- Hide the strips around the activity area (weigh them down with sticks and stones if it is windy).
- Make thirty copies of a simple 'Wanted!' poster template (or use blank sheets with older children).
- Write this message on your whiteboard: S'EREHT REHTONA RETTEL GNITIAW!
- Gather together any other resources required.

Session plan

1. Discover and decode the latest message on the board. Before leaving to find the letter, recap what has happened so far. Use talk partners to let the children remind each other how this adventure started, why the detectives wanted them to help, who the suspects are, and what the children think the suspects were poised to do at the end of the last session.
2. Nominate a child to find the latest letter. Seat the children at the edge of the activity area and read the letter aloud, checking for understanding.

3. Send the children into the activity area to find the information about Plonk and Snifter. As they gather it, Blu-Tack it to two sheets of sugar paper, one labelled 'Plonk' and the other labelled 'Snifter'. (The different font styles should help the children to work out which is which.)
4. Blu-Tack the fact sheets to a tree or wall so that all the children can refer to them. Ask the children to help read out the information so everyone can hear what it says. Ask the children to decide which one they are going to make a 'Wanted!' poster for, and discuss with a friend how they will draw them.
5. Hand out clipboards, pencils and rubbers so that the children can start work on their 'Wanted!' posters. As they finish, give them some Blu-Tack so they can put their posters up around the activity area. When all the children are finished, give them some time to wander around and view each other's efforts. The posters can be collected in at the end of the session or left in the activity area for Perks and Malik to collect later, as you see fit.
6. Pack up and return to the classroom.

Follow-up activity

Step 1: Update the woodland wall with photos and some posters.

Step 2: In groups, the children create word banks to describe one of the four characters: Mrs Beattie, the Reverend Grimsby, Ron Plonk and Archie Snifter.

Tips

ICT: Use the whiteboard to write the coded message.

Behaviour management: To give more children the chance to find a strip of paper, suggest that as soon as someone finds a fact, they stick it on the sugar paper and then sit down.

Simplify: The 'Wanted!' poster could be an artist's impression of the character, with just a few simple words and sentences underneath.

Extend: Encourage your class to use a wide range of interesting adjectives and verbs to describe the appearance and behaviour of their suspect.

Session 4: An eyewitness account

The children witness a bizarre event and, following the discovery of some stolen goods and the latest note from Perks and Malik, combine these sources to produce an eyewitness account of what they have seen.

Resources

Teacher

- Two people to act out the roles of Plonk and Snifter
- Two woolly hats and large coats/scarves
- A bag full of 'stolen goods' taken from a church, e.g. metal candlesticks, goblets, embroidered silk, hand-tooled metal picture frames – whatever you can find!
- A spade or trowel
- Writing frames (T4W1) for making an eyewitness account
- Clipboards and pencils
- Sugar-paper writing frame if doing a shared write
- Blu-Tack
- Digital camera

Book

- Appendix T4L4 (letter)
- Appendices T4E1 and T4E2
- Appendix T4W1

Preparation

- Photocopy the letter and hide it in the activity area as usual.
- Refer to Appendix T4W1 for a suggested layout for an eyewitness statement writing frame, and amend/make copies as necessary. If you are doing a shared write, make a large version on sugar paper.
- Make one copy each of T4E1 and T4E2, and give to one of your actors.
- Brief your actors on what to do, get them to practise so that they are confident, and agree on a sign from you for them to start (see 'Plan for the actors' below for more details).
- Stick a small label with 'RP' written on it to one of the scarves, and 'AS' to the other.
- Give your actors the bag of stolen goods and the spade/trowel.
- Write ENO EROM EGASSEM! on the board.
- Gather up any other resources required.

Session plan

Plan for the actors

- Tell your actors which direction you will be coming from so they can look out for you.
- Agree a signal, such as you shading your eyes from the sun with your hand, for them to start their performance.
- As they start, shush your class and gesture to them to stop, whispering to them to look at what's happening in the activity area.
- Upon the signal, both throw their scarves on the ground, wiping their brows. Snifter needs to mime digging a hole for the stolen goods, and Plonk needs to be reading the witness reports.
- Snifter will say things like: 'This is a good place for the stuff! Those horrible kids won't think of looking here. We can collect it later.'
- Plonk, looking worried, needs to say something like: 'Snifter, have you read these? The Rev's told them everything! We're finished!'
- They suddenly look up and notice your class watching them, scream, drop everything that they're holding and run off.

General session plan

1. Decode the latest message on the board, and before leaving recap the adventure so far. What discoveries are the children expecting to make this session?
2. As you approach the activity area, ensure that you are at the front and make the agreed signal for the actors to start. Immediately shush your class, urgently gesturing for them to stop where they are and watch.
3. Once the actors have run off, go into the activity area with your class and let them run around, collecting up what has been left behind. Make sure that someone has found the latest letter from Perks and Malik, then seat your class in a circle. Ask them briefly what they think just happened, and let them share their ideas. Read the latest letter aloud and check for understanding.
4. Suggest to the children that you all examine each of the items found in more detail by inviting a child to come up and describe it to the rest of the class. Use this as a way to draw in easily distracted children by giving them this key role. In particular, get them to find the initials on the scarves to make the link between Plonk and Snifter, and to speculate on where the stolen goods look like they might have come from.
5. Invite two of your more able children to read the eyewitness statements by Reverend Grimsby and Mrs Beattie that Plonk was worried about (these are Appendices T4E1 and T4E2). Use talk partners to let the children come to their conclusion about what

has just happened and whom they just saw. Ask them what they think they should do next. Agree that they should write eyewitness reports for Perks and Malik, as they mentioned in their letter.

6. If you want to do a shared write, stick up a sugar-paper version of an eyewitness report and let the children discuss each section with talk partners before feeding back to you. If you want them to work in pairs/groups/individually, hand out clipboards and writing frames.
7. Once the eyewitness accounts are finished, let the children read them to each other before leaving them in the same place where you find the letters from Perks and Malik.

Follow-up activity

Step 1: Update the woodland wall with photos and a few examples of eyewitness statements.

Step 2: Make a word bank of the interesting vocabulary used in the eyewitness statements to describe what the children saw.

Tips

ICT: Write the coded message on the interactive whiteboard.

Behaviour management: The main thing for this session is to ensure that your class do not go running into the activity area while the actors are there, or yell out: 'That's Ryan from Class 14!' Keep your class at quite a distance from the activity area, and prime them by saying, 'I think we should keep our wits about us when we go out there today.' Let the children enjoy the moment of stumbling upon the scene and finding the discarded items. The more involved they are in the discovery, the more the experience will belong to them and the more motivated they will be to complete their eyewitness accounts.

Simplify: Produce the eyewitness account as a shared write.

Extend: Produce the eyewitness accounts individually. Encourage the children to come up with descriptive verbs such as *roared* or *scuttled*.

Session 5: The final crime report

Do a final favour for Perks and Malik by writing up a crime report that they can hand in to their bosses.

Resources

Teacher

- Clipboards, pencils etc. if writing outside
- Digital camera

Book

- Appendix T4L5 (final letter)
- Appendix T4W2 or T4W3

Preparation

- Copy the final letter and place it in the activity area as usual.
- Crime reports are not, as yet, a writing genre of the Primary Literacy Strategy! Take a look at suggested writing frames T4W2 and T4W3, and adapt to fit your requirements – feel free to change as much as you require.
- A large sugar-paper writing frame, if you want to model how to fill it in.
- Blu-Tack.
- Write the following message on the board: KO, SIHT YLLAER SI EHT TSAL ENO.
- Gather up any other resources required.

Session plan

1. Notice and decode the latest message. Recap the adventures of the last session and ask the children what they think Perks and Malik will want our help with now.
2. Nominate a child to find the letter; seat the class and read it aloud. Check for understanding.
3. Ask the class to speculate on what a crime report is like. What kind of information would you include? Who will need to read it? (Suggest a solicitor or police officer.) Use talk partners to share ideas.
4. If you want to model how to fill in the crime report, do so now. Show the children the large sugar-paper version and let them discuss what to write in each section. Encourage them to give examples of interesting vocabulary that they could use.
5. The children complete their crime reports. Move around the group, making sure that they have the things they need to work without distraction. Put your teaching assistant with a small group of children who need encouragement to get started, and keep

returning to read their efforts and show interest in their ideas. You can treat this as a first draft or the finished article, depending on your requirements.

6. When everyone has finished, tidy up and return to the classroom.

Follow-up activity

Step 1: Update the woodland wall.

Step 2: In pairs, the children read each other their crime reports, and comment on good word choices/phrases.

Tips

ICT: Write the coded message on the interactive whiteboard.

Behaviour management: You might find it easier to preserve a peaceful working atmosphere if you send a group of early finishers back to the classroom with the teaching assistant.

Simplify: Choose the simpler writing frame for the crime report, or even just let the children draw a picture and then write an account underneath in their own words; go with what suits your class.

Extend: Choose the more complex writing frame and stress the need for as much detail as possible, including facial expressions, utterances, times of day/night, etc. There is nothing to stop you shoehorning in a recent teaching point that you want the class to revise, either!

8 Topic 5: Celtic life

Summary

Learn more about Celtic life with your guides from the Iceni warrior tribe, Brina and Caedmon.

Guidance

Narrative device: Letters.

Characters: A girl called Brina, meaning 'protector' and a boy called Caedmon, meaning 'wise warrior'.

Activity summary: Making miniature roundhouses, making replica swords for sacrifice to the gods, creating natural dyes, learning about the Green Man myth and making his likeness.

Resources

The basics

- Straw, twigs, sticks, clay, soil, scissors and string
- Clay modelling boards/plastic trays if making individual roundhouses
- Ingredients to make 'daub' out of soil, clay, water and grass clippings (to replace the animal dung)
- Sticks, foil, glue sticks, natural materials such as flowers, leaves etc. to decorate swords (you may want to use cardboard 'sword' outlines for younger children)
- Beads and feathers to decorate the replica swords
- Clay and plenty of leaves and other natural materials for creating the Green Man
- Flowers, weeds, leaves, soil, berries etc. for making natural dyes
- Palettes and stones for crushing up the materials
- Squares of white paper or fabric for testing out the dyes
- Paintbrushes and water
- Plenty of water for rinsing hands
- Two buckets
- Wet-wipes and paper towels

- Long length of string and pegs/paperclips (one per child)
- Bin bag

Wow factor

This is an easy topic to get carried away with!

- Instead of making individual models, make a miniature roundhouse community in the activity area; let the children poke sticks into the soil, wrap grasses around them and then coat with 'daub' before making the roofs and a surrounding palisade fence out of sticks
- Gold and silver pens to create tracery effects on the replica swords (please note that these pens will probably be ruined by the end of the session)
- A Green Man face that you have created somewhere in the activity area before the session, which the children can go and find
- For the dyes, juicy berries such as blackberries and raspberries, and brightly coloured flowers from your garden or an ageing bunch of flowers, such as marigolds, dahlias etc.

  NB: For safety, do NOT include any non-edible berries such as those found on deadly nightshade or yew trees. If in doubt, leave it out!

Writing outcome

A report about Celtic life, including information about the beliefs, rituals and home life of the Celts.

Follow-up activities

There is no communication with the characters after each session; instead, children will communicate with each other in pairs and groups to discuss their learning and speculate upon different theories about how the Celts lived.

Curricular links

History/Non-chronological reports (Literacy).

Author's comments

This topic involves mud, clay and natural dyes and has the potential to be very messy! Your class will LOVE it. If you have a high tolerance for mess and chaos, ask the children to wear art overalls so their uniforms aren't plastered in detritus before you notice it. If your tolerance of mess is low, you can still enjoy this topic by carefully limiting their activities.

You will really improve your class's understanding of what is required by making your own model roundhouse in advance. If this is not possible, ensure that they can look at pictures to see what you mean.

This topic works best in spring, summer or early autumn.

Session 1: Making a roundhouse

Meet Caedmon and Brina, your guides to Celtic life and beliefs, and make a miniature roundhouse.

Resources

Teacher

- Plenty of straw (buy a bale from a pet shop) and twigs, sticks, modelling clay, soil, scissors and string or small elastic bands
- A bucket for mixing the daub
- A 1-litre plastic bottle or other container filled with water
- Clay modelling boards/plastic trays if making individual roundhouses
- Designated area if making a roundhouse settlement
- Trowels/a gardening fork
- Pictures of an Iron Age roundhouse (try an image search on the internet)
- If you have time, make a model yourself, to show to the class
- A bucket of water for washing hands and some wet-wipes/paper towels
- Digital camera

Book

- Appendix T5L1 (first letter)

Preparation

- Photocopy the letter from Caedmon and Brina.
- Fold it and tuck it into a crook in a tree branch or under a stone, so that it looks as if it has been partially hidden.
- If you have time to make or start making a miniature roundhouse yourself, do so now!
- If making a settlement, dig over the soil in the designated area to loosen it, so that the children can easily poke sticks into it.
- Gather up the other materials needed.

Session plan

1. Tell the children that you thought you saw someone moving around in the activity area today before school started, and you were wondering who it was. Say that it looked like a little boy and a girl, but they were wearing unusual clothes so it was hard to tell. Ask your class if they will come outside with you now and just check that everything is as it should be in there.
2. As you approach the activity area, ask your class to walk carefully around it, looking for anything unusual. When someone finds the letter, call the class together and sit them down before reading it aloud. Check for understanding and any other knowledge about the Celts among your class.
3. Ask if anyone has seen a roundhouse before, and if so encourage them to describe its shape and what it was made of. Show the children either the pictures you have found or the model you have made, and re-read the relevant parts of Brina and Caedmon's letter. Talk about wattle and daub, and what they are both made from. To make your own daub, mix some clay, soil, grass clippings and water together in a bucket, inviting the children to come and mix it with a stick. Judge the consistency and add more of the various ingredients to get it right.

   At this point, you will need to clearly state which type of roundhouse your class is going to make: individual ones in trays/on modelling boards, or roundhouses in a 'settlement' that are dug into the soil.

4. **Individual roundhouses:** Hand out a modelling board to each child and roll out a sausage of clay before laying it in a ring shape on the board. Push twigs into the clay ring so that they stand upright, snapping them in two to make them roughly the same height. If you want to, thread some grasses through the twigs to imitate the woven wood or the wattle. Now take a handful of daub and coat the walls with it. Let the children get started on this, and then have your teaching assistant or yourself on hand to show groups of children how to make the roof when they are ready.
   Roundhouse settlement: As above, but instead of using a ring of clay to stabilise the wattle, the children will poke their sticks into the ground in a rough circle shape, building their roundhouses in the ground. If you have time after making the roofs, add a ring of sticks around the edge of the settlement to mimic the palisade fence built by the Celts to defend their territory.
5. To make the roof, take a handful of straw and pull all the strands in the same direction, like a pony's tail. Trim the ends so they are all the same length, and then fasten at one end with a small elastic band or some string. Splay the other end and balance it on top of the roundhouse walls to make a conical thatched roof. If the roof seems too thin, remove the elastic band and add more straw.
6. As the children finish, let them wash their hands in the bucket of water and wipe with

wet-wipes/paper towels. Let the children review their work by describing to each other in pairs what they have built, and how.

7. Tidy up and go back to the classroom. Ensure that all children wash their hands with soap and water.

Follow-up activity

Step 1: Update the woodland wall with photos of the children's roundhouses and images sourced from the internet, if available.

Step 2: Tell the children that Celtic hill-forts were given this name because they were always found at the top of high hills. They were often surrounded by green fields. In groups, ask the children to think about why this would have been a useful place to build their fort, and what they might have used the land around the hill-fort for. Ask the children to share their ideas with the rest of the class, following discussion.

Tips

ICT: Take plenty of photos of the roundhouses that the children make. You may want to make a video of one group presenting their ideas in Step 2 (see above) and then show it to the class on the interactive whiteboard.

Behaviour management: This is going to be a messy session, so make sure that you have the means to clean the worst of the mud off the children's hands before trooping back inside. It will also be great fun and the children will love it. Choose in advance whether to pair children up or let them work individually, but try to ensure that no child who is likely to become easily discouraged is left working alone. If creating a settlement, choose a wide area so that there is enough room for the children to sit and squat without crushing each other's efforts.

Simplify: Make bundles of straw in advance, so that all the children have to do is trim the ends and then splay to place on the walls. Let the children work in pairs to support each other with any fiddly bits.

Extend: Encourage your class to find a way of creating 'true wattle' by threading long grasses, green twigs or straw through the upright twigs before coating it in daub. (By green twigs I mean ones that have been freshly pulled from a tree/bush, so that they are still flexible.)

Session 2: Sacrifices to the gods

Find out about some of the many Celtic gods and goddesses before making a replica sword to be sacrificed in the river.

Resources

Teacher

- Supply of long sticks, enough for one per child
- Sword-shaped pieces of cardboard for younger children
- Foil to cover the swords
- Beads, feathers, flowers, leaves, strands of coloured wool for decoration
- Silver and gold pens (if you have them)
- Glue sticks
- Digital camera

Book

- Appendix T5L2 (second letter)

Preparation

- Photocopy the latest letter and leave it in the activity area in the same place as last time.
- Gather together all of the other materials required.
- Ensure that a good supply of natural materials is in the activity area.

Session plan

1. Remind the children about your adventures last week making roundhouses. What have they learned about what it's like to make one? Have they found out anything else since about life in Celtic times? Let the children discuss their ideas with each other and then share with the class.
2. Tell them that you think another letter is waiting in the activity area. Choose someone to go and look for it, and then seat the class and read it aloud. Check for understanding.
3. Talk to the class briefly about the way that the Celts would sacrifice either their best fighting sword or a replica made from wood. Explain what 'replica' means and talk about which kind of sword might have been better to please the gods with, and why.
4. Show the children what materials are available for making their swords, and then just let them get on with it. Remind them before starting about acceptable behaviour, e.g. no waving sticks around in each other's faces.

5. As the children finish, ask them to move around the site looking for useful or interesting things that someone else could add to their sword.
6. As a review, ask the children to look at their swords and think about what the decorations on their swords represent. Give them some ideas, such as: *this feather means that the person using it will think it's as light as a feather so they can carry it for miles* or *the feather represents the person using the sword being able to fly through the air when they jump*. They can then find a partner and tell them.
7. If you have access to a school pond, you can sacrifice your swords! Otherwise, bring them back to the classroom to use on the woodland wall.

Follow-up activity

Step 1: Update the woodland wall with photos and examples of the replica swords.

Step 2: Tell the children about Cernunos, the god of harvest. What kinds of things do you think would be offered to him? And why did they need to have a goddess of water called Sabrina? Let the children discuss their ideas in groups, with the teacher/teaching assistant filming one group's discussion on a digital camera. Upload for a plenary and watch as a class on the interactive whiteboard, inviting further comments from the class.

Tips

ICT: Take photos of the activities outside, and make a video of one group discussing their ideas (see Step 2 above).

Behaviour management: The key to this session running smoothly is setting very clear rules and expectations about how the children move around the site with their swords. Be as draconian as you feel is appropriate for your class; you know them best.

Simplify: Use cardboard outlines of swords that the children can stick interesting things onto.

Extend: Encourage the children to add Celtic-style tracery to their swords, using silver and gold pens or coloured pencils.

Session 3: The Green Man

Learn about the legend of the Green Man from Brina and Caedmon, and try to create your own Green Man.

Resources

Teacher

- Plenty of natural materials such as leaves, twigs, sticks, berries, weeds etc.
- Clay (enough for a small ball for each child)
- A small dish of water
- Two or three images of Green Men from the internet, printed off in colour
- Blu-Tack
- If you have time, your own simple Green Man (see below for ideas)
- Wet-wipes and a bucket of water for rinsing hands
- Paper towels
- Digital camera

Book

- Appendix T5L3 (letter)

Preparation

- Photocopy the latest letter, fold it and hide it in the activity area.
- Affix the Green Man pictures from the internet around the activity area, trying to position them so that the children will not see them from where they sit when listening to the latest letter.
- Create a Green Man somewhere in the activity area, either by sticking a small ball of clay onto a tree trunk and adding facial features using leaves, sticks, berries etc., or by making a face on the ground out of natural materials. This is for the children to discover, so try to position it away from where you will sit them down to read the letter.
- Gather up any other materials needed.

Session plan

1. Let the children know that you think another letter has appeared in the activity area. Before leaving, use talk partners to recap what they have learned so far about how

roundhouses were built and how important the gods and goddesses were to the Celts. Invite contributions from children who have found out further information.

2. Nominate a child to find the latest letter, seat the children and read it aloud. Check for understanding.
3. Re-read the part of the letter where Caedmon and Brina are inviting the children to look and listen carefully for the Green Man. Without moving from their places, can the children see anything that a Celt might have thought was evidence of the Green Man? Invite comments and ideas from the class.
4. Let the children explore the activity area, looking for further clues or signs of the Green Man. As each Green Man is discovered, call the other children over to take a look. Explain that the pictures from the internet might show a carving of the Green Man from stone, but note the leaf motifs around his head/face. Finish up in front of the Green Man that you have created from clay and natural materials on a tree trunk (if you did not have time, don't worry – just model how to make one in front of them now).
5. Explain that in a moment the children will be creating their own Green Man. Give them a few minutes to discuss their ideas about what they will use for the hair/eyes/ears/beard/mouth/nose. If you do not have many trees or trunks, the children can make collages of the Green Man on the ground, or model the clay on stones/the ground. Provide a small dish of water for children to use to soften the clay if it's very hard.
6. Once the children have finished creating their Green Men, review the work by going 'on tour' around the activity area, with each child stepping forward to explain their design. Alternatively, try sitting the class down and sending half at a time to walk around the activity area, quietly looking at all the faces. Then let them sit in pairs and talk about their favourite Green Man and what they liked about it.
7. Take plenty of photos of the Green Man designs, tidy up and return to the classroom.

Follow-up activity

Step 1: Update the woodland wall with photos of the Green Men and the images from the internet.

Step 2: Model how to make a spidergram of 'how life was different for the Celts', and then ask the children to work in pairs or small groups to create their own spidergram on sugar paper. The idea is to get them to summarise and articulate their learning so far, while also drawing out other aspects that have not been explicitly covered by the topic but the children have nevertheless inferred, e.g. *it was very dark at night because they had no lights* or *they made their own clothes because there were no shops.* Ask the children to present their spidergrams briefly to the class and then add them to the woodland wall.

Tips

ICT: Take photos of the activities outside, and then make a video of one group explaining their ideas (see Step 2) to watch on the interactive whiteboard.

Behaviour management: Take plenty of water for rinsing and wet-wipes outside, as the children will have clay on their hands by the end of the activity. You may find that the children finish this activity quite quickly. If so, ask them to think of an offering suitable for the Green Man that would bring a good harvest, and to see if they can find something to symbolise it that they can add to their Green Man.

Simplify: If the clay is very hard, show the children how to roll it between their hands to soften it. You may also want to put your teaching assistant in charge of tearing off balls of clay for the children.

Extend: Encourage the children to add more detail to their faces by carving marks into the clay with twigs.

Session 4: Making natural dyes

Use natural materials to experiment with making dyes, and test them out on squares of cloth.

Resources

Teacher

- Pencils
- Thirty squares of cloth for testing out dyes (if you don't have any, use squares of paper)
- One paint palette per child
- Smooth stones or sticks for mixing dyes
- Plenty of natural materials for creating dyes: young leaves, flowers, grass clippings, weeds, berries, chalk dust, bark. Feel free to bring in blackberries or elderberries, old bunches of brightly coloured flowers, nettle roots and anything else that you think might make an interesting colour when crushed
- Wet-wipes, bucket of water for rinsing hands and paper towels
- Paint brushes of varying thicknesses
- Long length of string and pegs/paperclips (one per child)
- A bin bag for carrying back the dirty palettes, brushes and paper towels
- Digital camera

Book

- Appendix T5L4 (letter)

Preparation

- Photocopy the latest letter, fold it and place it in the activity area.
- Cut up squares of cloth/paper for testing the dyes.
- Add whatever materials that you have brought from home to the activity area; you may wish to partially conceal them so the children can discover them as they look around, or just lay them all out in trays.

While raiding your back garden for supplies, make sure that you do not include berries from the deadly nightshade plant, yew tree or anything else that you are not sure about.

- Gather up any other materials required.

Session plan

1. Let the children know that another letter has appeared in the activity area. Before leaving the classroom, recap what they have learned so far, including last week's adventure making their own Green Man.
2. Nominate someone to find the letter, seat the children and read it aloud. Check for understanding and reassure the children that they will not be using the more unpleasant ingredients to make their dyes!
3. Show the children what they will have to create their dyes: a palette for collecting materials and a stone or stick for crushing them up. Indicate clearly and unambiguously any areas or materials that you do NOT want them to use (for example, if you have a yew tree encroaching on the activity area, the children need to know that the berries are poisonous). Also, make it very clear that no one should put any of the materials in their mouths – this will be particularly important if they will be using recognisable fruits such as raspberries.

   If you have mushrooms or fungi growing in your area, advise your class not to use them at all.

4. Before starting to make the dyes, hand out a square of fabric/paper to each child and ask them all to write their initials in the corner (the teaching assistant can do this in advance if you wish).
5. Let the children make their dyes by crushing and mixing the materials in their palettes with sticks and stones. Move around the site supervising them and ensuring that the children are remembering the rules for safe use that you outlined earlier.
6. If you don't want the children to get their hands *too* dirty, they can use paintbrushes to transfer their dyes to the testing squares. Alternatively, let them try to make their own brushes from grass and sticks, or use their fingers. Whichever way you slice it, this will be a messy session, but be comfortable in the knowledge that a huge amount of fun and first-hand learning are taking place! Ask the children to rinse their hands in the bucket of water when finished.
7. While the class are busy making and testing their dyes, make a 'washing line' for pegging up the samples by tying a length of string between two trees. As the children finish, get them to peg their sample squares to the line (make sure it is low enough for them to do so). When all the children have finished, they can take it in turns to tell their peers about their dyes and how they created them.
8. While this is taking place, ask your teaching assistant to dip each palette in the bucket of water, rinsing off the worst mess before throwing it into the bin-bag for carrying back to the classroom. If you have used paintbrushes, you can also give these an initial rinse before washing them properly in the classroom.
9. Before returning to the classroom, ensure that all children have rinsed and wiped their hands, and make sure they all wash their hands with soap upon return to the school building.

Follow-up activity

Step 1: Update the woodland wall with photos of the activity and some testing squares.

Step 2: Ask the children to take a coloured pencil, any colour at all, and then to think about what they could use to create a dye of that colour. They can come up with things they did not use during the session, e.g. blood for brown, coal dust for black, daffodils for yellow. Share ideas with the rest of the class.

Tips

ICT: Take plenty of photos and add to the woodland wall.

Behaviour management: This session involves some cleaning up afterwards, but you should be able to find some volunteers who will wash all the palettes and paintbrushes. If you have some children finishing early, occupy them with helping their friends to find interesting materials.

Simplify: You know your class best, so if you don't think that they can cope with using edible fruits without popping them into their mouths, don't supply them. Ask the children to use paintbrushes to transfer the dyes to the testing square.

Extend: Encourage the children to make their own paintbrushes to transfer the dye.

Session 5: Writing a book about Celtic life

Help Caedmon and Brina to pass on their knowledge about life in Celtic times to other children by making a book of reports.

Resources

Teacher

- Clipboards, paper and pencils if working outside
- Writing frames with subject headings already specified (if appropriate)
- Eight sheets of sugar paper and felt-tip pens
- Blu-Tack
- Digital camera

Book

- Appendix T5L5 (final letter)

Preparation

- Photocopy and fold the latest letter and place it in the activity area.
- Gather up any other materials required.

Session plan

1. Tell the children that there is another letter in the activity area, although you have a feeling that it may be the last. Before leaving, recap on what they have learned so far about Celtic life and beliefs by sitting the children in a circle and letting them take turns to mime an aspect, so the others can guess what it is, e.g. *sacrificing a sword to win a battle, cooking over a fire.* Encourage a wide range of contributions.
2. Nominate a child to find the latest letter, seat the children and then it read aloud. Check for understanding.
3. Give the children a few minutes to discuss in pairs what they would include in any report about the Celts (this does not have to be subject headings – for younger children it could just be facts). Invite contributions, summarising them into subject headings as you go, if you want the reports to be laid out this way, e.g. *So we could put those ideas about painting woad on their faces and wearing clothes coloured with natural dyes in a section called 'Appearance', couldn't we?*
4. Put the children into eight small groups and give each group one of the previous session themes to discuss; you will have two groups for each session theme. They will make a

mind-map of all the ideas they have for that session theme. Then move the groups around so that each one can work on a different mind-map. Ask the children in each group to read the mind-map to each other and then add to it any further ideas that they may have. Continue until each group has read and contributed to a mind-map on each session theme (this means that they will set one up, and then annotate three more).

5. If you are writing the reports outside, stick the mind-maps up around the activity area so that the children can refer to them. If returning to the classroom, put them up inside.
6. The children complete their reports. Ensure that they are comfortable – if it's too cold outside for sitting and writing, move them all back inside but let them keep the clipboards as they will enjoy using them for their work.
7. Move around the group, singling out children who need encouragement as they write, reading excerpts aloud and praising their ideas. Ensure that there are enough rubbers and so on that the children can remain on task.
8. When finished, let the children read their reports to each other in pairs, and then swap and read again.

Follow-up activity

Step 1: Update the woodland wall with photos of the children writing their reports and examples of them. If you want to use these pieces of writing as a draft, ask the children to edit their work by checking for missing or incorrect punctuation, spellings etc.

Step 2: Create a book by putting the reports into a ring binder with some photos on the cover of the artefacts made by the children during the topic. This can then be shared with other classes in the school.

Tips

ICT: If you have a visualiser or projector, you can use this to show the children's work on the interactive whiteboard and read it together, singling out particular features for praise.

Behaviour management: If your class are not very familiar with the non-chronological report format, you will find it easier to teach these features prior to the children doing this piece of writing.

Simplify: Model how to make a report by doing a shared write on the interactive whiteboard; then let the children produce their own versions.

Extend: Recap the features of report writing that you want to see included – sub-headings, introductions, paragraphs, bulleted or numbered lists – and encourage the children to use them. Include teaching points from recent Literacy lessons as appropriate.

9 Topic 6: Animal world

Summary

Learn more about native animals from a friendly squirrel and song thrush, and help them choose suitable neighbours.

Guidance

Narrative device: Letters, hidden in the same place in the activity area.

Characters: A song thrush and squirrel will introduce your class to some of the other animals living in the local area.

Activity summary: A range of information-finding and sorting games and recording, including: jigsaws, Eyes and Brain, True/False Trees, making posters, and also making nests.

Resources

The basics

- Images from the internet, enlarged and printed
- Sugar paper, plain paper, pencils, marker pens, rubbers
- Clipboards
- Blu-Tack
- Coloured pencils
- A3 coloured card/sugar paper in four different colours

Wow factor

- Any enhancement of the activity area with traces of the animals being studied, such as a nest, footprints or samples of the food that the animals eat, would increase the children's excitement and interest. Let your imagination run wild, subject to the usual time constraints!
- A selection of library books about the animals being studied, for the children to look at in the Book Corner

– provide a range of reading levels by asking the class teachers of older/younger year groups if you can borrow theirs.

Writing outcome

A non-chronological report about local animals.

Follow-up activities

Creation of fact banks on the woodland wall about the different animals that the children are learning about.

Curricular links

This can be linked to Science or Geography topics that look at animals in the local environment.

Author's comments

This topic lets your class discover information about various animals that live in the UK, but feel free to change them for creatures more specific to your local environment. (If you do this, make sure that you have checked and amended the relevant appendices.)

The learning in this topic is predominantly games based, so it is suitable for any time of year.

The appendices for this topic are differentiated, so don't be put off by the lengthy lists in the session plans – just choose the ones best for your class. As ever, amend or enhance them as you see fit.

Session 1: Welcome to our world

Two friendly local animals invite you to discover more about them and where they live.

Resources

Teacher

- Two A4 colour posters of a song thrush and two of a grey squirrel (see 'ICT skills' in Chapter 10 for guidance)
- Four sheets of plain A4 paper
- Four clipboards, pencils and rubbers
- A scruffy, handwritten note that says 'Look under the [insert name] tree!'
- Blu-Tack
- A handful of soil
- Digital camera

Book

- Introduction letter (Appendix T6L1)
- Two copies of the fact file for each animal (Appendices T6F1 and T6F2 are simple facts for younger children. Appendices T6F3 and T6F4 contain some lies for older children to spot.)

Preparation

- Photocopy the introduction letter, roll it up and tie it with string.
- Choose which pair of fact files to use, and photocopy two copies of each. Roll them up and tie with string.
- Print off two coloured posters of a squirrel and two of a song thrush.
- Put the handwritten note on your desk and scatter a bit of soil on it.
- Go to the activity area and place the introduction letter under the tree mentioned on the scruffy note.
- Hide each of the fact files within the activity area.
- Find a suitable place to stick up the posters for Brain and Eyes. Choose the area where the person being the Brain will sit, and ensure that they cannot see the animal posters from that location (see 'Games and activities' in Chapter 10 for guidance on how to play).
- Gather together all other materials needed.

Session plan

1. Affecting annoyance, ask the children who has left this scruffy little note on your desk, and a handful of soil into the bargain? Allow yourself to be persuaded by your class's indignant response that it wasn't them. Read it aloud and decide that maybe you should go and take a look under the tree, as the note requests.
2. Either discover the note hidden in the activity area as a group, or send a child ahead with the teaching assistant to discover it. Sit your class in the activity area and read the note. Ask them if they are ready to find out which animals sent us this letter, and divide the class into four teams to play Brain and Eyes. See 'Games and activities' in Chapter 10 for guidance on how to play.
3. Describe how to play Brain and Eyes, and nominate one child in each group to be the Brain. The rest will take it in turns to be the Eyes. Give the Brains a piece of paper on a clipboard, a pencil and a rubber. Sit them in a position where they cannot see what the other Brains are drawing, or the location of the posters that the Eyes will be looking at.
4. Prepare the teams to start by telling each team where their poster is. Play the game of Brain and Eyes, and afterwards gather the class together to compare the pictures drawn; agree on the identity of the two animals who wrote the note.
5. Once the identity of the animals has been established, complete the next challenge in the letter, which is to find out more about them. Explain that there are four fact files hidden in the activity area. Each group has to find one, and then read it together. To give them a chance to run around, let the child who was the Brain in each group do the searching.
6. If you have chosen the fact files with lies, give the groups time to read through and cross out the items that they think can't be true. Discuss which ones are correct as a class, so that all children learn about both animals.
7. For the review, children select a partner and one of the animals studied, and then take it in turns to tell each other a fact about it. Draw out their responses by asking the following questions: *Do you know anything extra? What did you notice about the way it looked and its size?* They then swap and do the other animal.
8. Tidy up and return to the classroom.

Follow-up activity

Step 1: In pairs, children can create a poster of one of the animals learned about today, annotating it with words and phrases.

Step 2: Update the woodland wall with pictures and posters from the day's activities.

Tips

ICT: Use a digital camera to record the children's activities and add pictures to the woodland wall.

Behaviour management: If Brain and Eyes seems chaotic the first time you play it, take heart. This will be a useful learning experience for playing it again later in the topic.

Simplify: Use the simple fact files and be on hand to help with reading any unfamiliar words.

Extend: Use the fact files that require the children to spot the deliberate lies. Ask them to share their ideas on which facts are false, and to justify their views. The Brain and Eyes games can also be made harder by cutting random shapes out of a piece of A4 paper and then placing it over the poster the Eyes will be looking at. The children will be unable to see the entire image at once and will have to guess what the hidden parts look like.

Session 2: Who else lives here?

Find out more about the other animals that live here by completing fact jigsaws and creating posters.

Resources

Teacher

- Paper, pencils/pens for creating posters (if the weather is rotten you may choose to do this back in the classroom)
- Clipboards, if you have them and are using A4 paper
- Blu-Tack
- Digital camera

Book

- Appendix T6L2 (letter)
- Jigsaws T6J1–T6J4, enlarged to A3 size and mounted on coloured card. Make sure each jigsaw is mounted on a different colour.

Preparation

- Photocopy and roll up the letter and tie it with string.
- Make A3-enlarged photocopies of the jigsaws in the appendices listed above and mount them on coloured card (put each jigsaw on a different colour, so the children can find the pieces they are looking for).
- Cut up the jigsaws and hide the pieces in the activity area.
- Place the letter from the animals under the same tree as last time.
- Gather any other materials needed.

Session plan

1. Tell the children that you think they should go and take a look at the activity area, as you think you saw another letter poking out from under the trees.
2. Before heading out, recap with the children what they have learned about the animals so far.
3. Find the letter and sit the children down at the edge of the activity area (this is to avoid them charging in and picking up the jigsaw pieces, but if your area is very large you could take them in). Read the letter and check that the children understand what they will be doing. Put the children in the same groups as last session, and give them all a colour to hunt for.

4. Children find the pieces of the jigsaws, complete the jigsaws on the grass and then read out the facts to each other. When all the jigsaws are finished, ask each group to feed back to the class about which animal they have found, and what they have learned about it. Be prepared to help younger children read some of the information.
5. Explain to the children that they will now make a poster of the animal they have learned about, so that they can put it up on the woodland wall in the classroom. Decide whether they will be working in groups or pairs, and hand out materials as appropriate (see 'Behaviour management' notes below).
6. Give children Blu-Tack so that they can stick their posters up around the site (e.g. on tree trunks, walls or a tarmac path) and create an animal gallery. Then let the children walk around, looking at each other's work and reading it.
7. Review: ask the children to comment on the following in pairs: *Which poster do you think would be best for someone in Reception, and why? Which poster would be useful for someone in Year 6, and why? Which of these animals might be friends with each other, and why?*
8. If possible, leave the posters up for the animals to look at once your class has left the area. Then bring them back later with a smudge on a corner of each one, from an interested animal's paw. If this is not possible, take them down and bring back to class.

Follow-up activity

Step 1: Update the woodland wall with a few posters or words about the new animals the children have discovered.

Step 2: Model how to create a simple table of similarities and differences between two of the animals they have learned about today. Let the children try to do this with two animals of their choosing, in pairs or small groups.

Tips

ICT: Use a digital camera to take pictures of the completed jigsaws, and of the animal gallery stuck to the trees, to add to the woodland wall.

Behaviour management: If your class are going to do poster work in groups, you will want at least A3-sized paper, if not sugar paper. Bear in mind that the larger the paper, the messier the work, as the children will not be able to find a flat surface outside. If working in pairs, ensure that you don't have two children together who both avoid writing; pair up reluctant writers with someone keen to scribe their ideas, so they will contribute.

Simplify: For very young classes, the children can draw pictures of the animals they learned about and then the teaching assistant can scribe their comments and descriptions of them for addition to the woodland wall in the classroom.

Extend: Once the groups have completed the jigsaws and discussed what they have found out, get the children to hide the pieces again and then give each team a different colour. Once they have completed this jigsaw, they then create a poster of the two animals they have done, showing similarities and differences.

Session 3: A new neighbour?

Hunt the facts and help the woodland friends to decide whether they should let a new animal move into their habitat.

Resources

Teacher

- String
- Blu-Tack
- Two large pieces of sugar paper, one with 'True' written at the top and the other with 'False' written at the top
- Clipboards
- Notepaper and pencils for writing letters
- Digital camera

Book

- Appendix T6L3 (letter)
- 1 copy of T6F5 (easier) or T6F6 (harder), enlarged and mounted on card

Preparation

- Photocopy the latest letter and tie it with string.
- Make an enlarged photocopy of T6F5/F6, mount it on card and then cut into pieces, with one fact on each piece.
- Place the letter in the usual place in the activity area.
- Hide the facts around the activity area, using a mix of ground-, shrub- and tree-level places. Weigh down with stones if windy.
- Stick the 'True' sugar paper to a tree/wall, and the 'False' sugar paper to another tree/wall nearby.
- Gather together all other materials needed.

Session plan

1. Tell the children that you think there may be another letter for them underneath the tree. Before leaving the classroom, look at the woodland wall and recap what has happened so far. Focus on what the class have learned about the different animals. In talk partners, the children describe one of the animals without saying its name, and their partner has to guess it. Then swap.
2. Upon arrival at the activity area, sit the children down and ask them if they can see or hear any of the animals. Then retrieve the letter and read it together.

3. Explain that the first thing they will do is look for facts about this potential new neighbour. Tell your class that the facts were hidden by the different animals, so they will have to look where they may have hidden them.
4. Play True/False Trees, with the children hunting for facts in pairs (note: there are fifteen different facts). See 'Games and activities' in Chapter 10 for an explanation of how to play.
5. Once the class have agreed which of the facts are true, put them in groups of five or six and ask them to discuss whether or not they think that the buzzard should move in. Regroup as a class and invite their comments. Draw out their answers with reference to the needs of the other animals and the buzzard.
6. Ask the children to write a letter to the animals, advising them of their decision. Encourage children to do this in pairs or threes, as this will maximise the amount of discussion and idea sharing that takes place. It's up to you whether you want to provide colouring pencils or crayons to decorate the letters.
7. The children have already reviewed their learning by composing a letter, so ask them to get together with another pair/group and read their letter aloud. The other pair/group will offer constructive feedback about what they liked about it (this can include presentational or explanatory elements such as *You made it look nice*, *You explained things clearly*). Once finished, the children leave the letters somewhere secret for the animals to find later.
8. Tidy up and return to the classroom.

Follow-up activity

Step 1: Update the woodland wall with the 'True' buzzard facts, copies of some letters and photos of the children.

Step 2: In pairs, the children create a mind-map of one particular animal, writing around the edges as many words as they can think of to describe it, e.g. *orange*, *furry*, *stealthy*, *carnivore.* Then they team up with another pair who did the same animal, and compare mind-maps.

Tips

ICT: Take digital photos of the children as they work outdoors and use them on the woodland wall.

Behaviour management: As ever, be on hand to help children read the facts and ensure that none of your writing pairs/groups is made up entirely of reluctant writers.

Simplify: Let the children write a really simple note, such as: 'The buzzard is bad because he will eat the rabbits.'

Extend: Draw out the children's discussion on why the buzzard would be a problem, beyond the obvious 'rabbit eating' fact. For example, note the typical habitat. Is this provided by your school? Extend their thoughts about mammals; what other animals might be at risk? Encourage the children to use a formal letter format for their response to the animals.

Session 4: A mysterious arrival

A lost creature turns up in the woods. Help the animals to decide what it is and whether it will fit in and how to make it feel at home.

Resources

Teacher

- Four A4 posters of a mole – try and find four different images on the internet
- Blu-Tack
- Four A4 sheets of paper, pencils and clipboards
- Natural materials, e.g. sticks, grass, stones, twigs, soil, leaves etc.
- Digital camera

Book

- Appendix T6L4 (letter)
- Appendix T6F7, enlarged if possible to A3

Preparation

- Photocopy the latest letter and tie it with string.
- Find four different pictures of moles on the internet, and create four A4 colour posters (see 'ICT skills' in Chapter 10 for guidance).
- Make a copy of Appendix T6F7, enlarged to A3 size, and roll it up and tie it with string.
- Put the letter under the tree as usual.
- Stick up the mole posters for Brain and Eyes.
- Hide the rolled up mole facts poster (T6F7) as high up as you can within the activity area, but within reach of a resourceful child.
- Gather up any other resources required.

Session plan

1. Tell the children that you have seen another letter from the animals in the activity area. Before setting out, recap the activities of the previous sessions, and which animals they have learned about. In pairs, ask one of the children to mime one of the animals while the other has to guess which one it is. Swap.
2. Upon arrival at the activity area, sit the children down and then find the letter and read it to them. Put the children in the same teams as before for Brain and Eyes, and position the Brains where they cannot see the posters that the Eyes will look at (choose a different person to be the Brain this session). Explain that you will play the game to

find out what type of animal this mysterious arrival might be. See 'Games and activities' in Chapter 10 for how to play this game.

3. Once the children have finished, ask them to decide in their groups which animal they think they have discovered, and to write any facts that they may already know about it around the edge of the picture that the Brain has drawn. Discuss these ideas as a class (you may want to sit them in a circle for this).
4. Explain that the animals have made a poster of what they found out from their mysterious animal before it fell asleep, and that the song thrush has hidden it. Send out the children who were the Brains to find it, and once they return, Blu-Tack it to a wall/tree so that the others can all gather round. The children volunteer to read out different facts to the rest of the class. Give the children five minutes in their groups to update their posters with any other facts that they want to add. They can then stick them up around the activity area.
5. In pairs, the children evaluate the information against the questions in the letter (you may need to remind them of these) and decide if the mole would be happy living there. Read out the last sentence again, and ask the children to build beds for the mole to recover on where the other animals can check up on him, i.e. not underground. Encourage creative ideas and the use of a wide range of materials.
6. The children review each other's work by going on a tour around the different nests, led by the teacher. At each nest, the children who built it step out to explain what they have made, and the thinking behind it.
7. Tidy up and return to the classroom.

Follow-up activity

Step 1: Update the woodland wall with pictures of the different nests and an example of the annotated posters created during Brain and Eyes.

Step 2: Put the children into groups and give each group an animal that they have learned about during this topic. Ask them, in ten minutes, to come up with a brief report about it, including any information that they have subsequently gleaned from information books or conversations with others. They then present their report to the rest of the class (they can do this orally or as a written poster, as you feel appropriate). This will give you the chance to identify any teaching points you need to cover before the final session, when they will write an individual report on a specific animal.

Tips

ICT: Take plenty of pictures of the nests that the children build, and add them to the woodland wall.

Behaviour management: Ensure that the children can remember the rules of Brain and Eyes before playing it again.

Simplify: You could simplify the game by using the same picture for all the children, and all the Eyes having to run to the same place to look at it (the Brains will still have to be sitting out of sight, however).

Extend: If you can find some information books about moles, either bring them out with you or make copies of specific pages. Give this information to each group during step 4 of the session, and ask them to read it to each other and annotate their drawing with any facts that they think are interesting.

Session 5: Help us to make a book!

Help any new arrivals in the woods to settle in by creating a book all about the other residents.

Resources

Teacher

- Paper, pencils, colouring pencils, clipboards for writing outside
- Writing frame as appropriate
- Six large sheets of sugar paper and dark-coloured whiteboard pens
- Blu-Tack
- Any information or fact books that you want to supply (see 'Extend' below)
- Digital camera

Book

- Appendix T6L5 (final letter)

Preparation

- Photocopy and tie up the latest letter.
- Place it under the tree.
- Gather up any writing materials and information that you want the children to use outside.

Session plan

1. Let the children know that another letter has turned up under the tree. Tell the children that you think this may be the last one. Go through each of the animals that they have learned about one by one, and ask the children to call out things they know about them, one at a time. Can your class find an animal that they can all give a separate fact for? (Start with shy or less-confident children, so that they are less likely to draw a blank further into the game.)
2. Go out to the activity area and seat the children. Read the letter. If you wish to model any features of the report, such as layout, subheadings etc., do so on a large sheet of sugar paper.
3. Ask the children to think about which animal they want to write about. Put them in groups and give each group a sheet of sugar paper on which to create a word bank of

useful vocabulary that they may want to use (although the primary purpose of this activity is to stimulate the children's ideas and prime their word choices, try to put a reasonably proficient speller in charge of recording these ideas in case they are copied down by others later on).

4. Share the ideas of each group briefly with the rest of the class and stick them up around the activity area using Blu-Tack.
5. Hand out the clipboards and writing materials for the children to start work on their report. Before they start, get each child to tell the child next to them what their first sentence will be.
6. Move around the site ensuring that the children have access to rubbers or rulers when they need them, encouraging children to get started. Praise early finishers for their efforts and use open questioning such as *Have you thought about . . .? What could you add about . . .? How could you explain . . .?* to elicit some ideas for further writing from them.
7. Gather up the materials and return to the classroom.

Follow-up activity

Step 1: Update the woodland wall with pictures and copies of the reports.

Step 2: If the work completed outdoors is being treated as a first draft, ask the children to swap papers with each other and, using a coloured pencil, carefully correct any errors noticed, e.g. punctuation, capitals, key word spellings. If it is final, give them the chance to read their work to each other.

Tips

ICT: Take pictures of the children writing and add them to the woodland wall.

Behaviour management: Never underestimate the number of rubbers that a class will need. For older children you may find it easier to have a 'rubber and ruler tree' where they borrow and return items. Place any children that you will need to continuously encourage close together so that they can hear your praise and discussions with their peers.

Simplify: A group could do a shared write of a report with the teaching assistant, and then copy it up afterwards. Alternatively, they could all do a shared write and then work independently on their own versions.

Extend: Ensure that your class is clear about your expectations for layout, content and organisation of work. Provide examples of information texts for them to look at and ask them to come up with a list of features that they think their reports should contain.

10 How do I . . .?

This chapter is organised in two parts. The first part explains how to do some of the things mentioned in the session plans, and is divided into 'Games and activities' and 'ICT skills'. The second part gives links and contact details for more information about resources, training, grants and so on.

Part 1: Games, activities and ICT skills

Games and activities

- How do I make a paper hat?
- How do I play Brain and Eyes?
- How do I play True/False Trees?
- How do I make a mud pool?
- How do I tie a pirate knot?

How do I make a paper hat?

You may already know this as the way to make a simple paper boat.

- Take a sheet of newspaper and crease it along the centre fold.
- Lay it down flat with the fold at the top.
- Now fold down each top corner diagonally, making the two halves of the folded edge meet. You now have a triangular shape with a narrow strip below it.
- Now fold up the bottom strip of paper, over the base of the triangle. Turn the paper over and turn up the bottom strip on the other side. Insert your hand to open up the triangle. You have a hat!

How do I play Brain and Eyes?

Put simply, the premise of this game is that a group of children (the Eyes) will take it in turns to look at a hidden poster, and then report back to another child (the Brain), who has not seen it but has to draw it.

- The positioning of the children is important in this game, as you want to keep the poster hidden so that the Brain is entirely reliant on the descriptions of the Eyes.
- In advance of playing, check your activity area and find enough suitable walls/trees to which to attach your posters, and enough suitable positions for the Brains; if you have to use a different part of the school grounds, this is fine.
- Divide the children into groups.
- Nominate a child to be the Brain – they will sit still and draw an approximation of what the Eyes describe to them.
- Sit each Brain in their position and describe the location of the hidden poster to the rest of their team.
- Explain to the Eyes that their job is not to merely say what the poster shows, but to describe it in sufficient detail that the Brain can create as accurate a drawing as possible.
- Send the Eyes (one child at a time) to look at the poster for thirty seconds, and then tell them when to run back to the Brain. Give each of the Eyes thirty seconds to describe what they have seen to the Brain before sending the next Eyes. Repeat as many times as needed, adjusting the timings to fit your class as required (you can make it harder by reducing the amount of time, and easier by increasing it).
- When finished, send the Brains to collect the posters that they had to draw, and then let the groups compare their collective efforts with the originals. Which features did they manage to describe and record well?

How do I play True/False Trees?

- Find two trees or, failing that, walls or slabs of tarmac at least two metres apart.
- Stick a large piece of sugar paper with 'True' written at the top of it on one, and stick a piece with 'False' written at the top of it on the other.
- See the session plan for details of what items the children will be sorting into 'true' and 'false', and make or copy as required.
- Give each child one of the items – for example, a slip of paper with a fact written on it about a particular animal – and explain that they have to decide if it is true or false.
- On an agreed signal from the teacher, the children take it in turns to stick their paper to the 'True' or 'False' tree.
- Once all the words or facts have been stuck onto the two trees, review them together. If some children cannot decide where to stick their papers, let them show them to the rest of the class and seek the advice of their peers.
- Increase the amount of movement by placing the True and False posters a good distance from where the children are waiting. You can also ask the children to run to and from the group.

How do I make a mud pool?

'Mud pool' is probably stretching it; you're basically making a small mud supply that the children can use.

- Choose a soil-covered area that children will not walk through, e.g. under a tree.
- Dig it over with a trowel or gardening fork to loosen the soil.
- Pour in some water and stir to achieve the desired consistency.
- Mark the edge of the mud pool with leaves so the children do not step in it by mistake.
- If you are concerned about mess or behaviour, ask your teaching assistant to supervise while the children come to collect mud in plastic cups, their hands or small spades.

How do I tie a pirate knot?

A pirate knot is simply the first stage of tying a shoelace, but done twice.

- Take both ends of a length of string and cross one over the other.
- Tuck one end under the other, pull it through the loop and pull to tighten.
- Repeat.
- Shout 'Aargggghhh!' like a pirate (optional).

ICT skills

- How can I edit session-letter content?
- How can I add a border to the letter to make it look more distinctive?
- How can I create bordered writing paper for the final writing task?
- How do I find and use images from the internet?
- How do I create a poster from an image found on the internet?
- How do I make a set of images to use on my interactive whiteboard?
- How can I find a sound-clip and play it through my classroom computer?
- How do I create free email accounts online for topic characters/my class?
- How can I make a voice recording on my computer?

How can I edit session-letter content?

You may be lucky enough to have software that recognises text from a scanned document. If so, scan in the letter you intend to use, and follow the instructions given by the software wizard. Ask your ICT co-ordinator if character-recognition software is installed on your computer.

For everyone else, the only way to edit the letter content is to first retype it in a word processor, such as Microsoft Word.

- Open a word processor document and type the session letter that you want to use.
- As you go, change the details to reflect the interests or experiences of your class, or to set a different activity.
- Save the document before printing it.

How can I add a border to the letter to make it look more distinctive?

Always choose the same border for letters for the same topic; this gives you the option of creating bordered writing paper for the final writing task that has the same decoration, thus reinforcing the link between the children's experiences and what they are about to write. The following instructions assume that your word processor is Microsoft Word.

- Open the document that you wish to add the border to in Word.
- If you are using a version of Word prior to 2007, go to Format, then Borders and Shading. Click Page Borders, and then select the type you require. Click OK to see it on the page. To see other border designs, repeat the steps above and the new design will replace the existing one.
- If you are using Word 2007 or later, go to the Home tab on the ribbon. The border options are in the Paragraph section of the Home tab.
- When you are happy with your border selection, save the document.

How can I create bordered writing paper for the final writing task?

- Open a document in Microsoft Word, type the date, title and a dotted line for the child's name. Then select a border type, following the instructions above for adding a border.
- Save and print.

How do I find and use images from the internet?

- Open your internet browser and type the URL of a search engine into the address bar, such as Google.
- Click on the 'images' tab, type your search query into the search engine and click on the search icon.
- When you find an image that you like, click on it to see the larger version, and then save it to your computer by right clicking on the image, selecting 'Save image as . . .' and saving.
- Save it to a folder on your computer.

How do I create a poster from an image found on the internet?

The following instructions assume that your word processor is Microsoft Word. There are also other methods for enlarging and printing image files that do not involve importing them into a word processor and that you may prefer to use if you are familiar with them.

- Find and save the image that you want to use, as above.
- Open a document in Microsoft Word.
- For versions of Word prior to 2007, go to Insert, then Picture, then From File.
- For Word 2007 or later, go to the Insert tab and click on Picture.
- In all versions of Word, now browse to the image that you want to use.
- Double-click on it to insert into the Word document.
- Click once on the image, so that it has a black border. Place your cursor in the bottom right corner of the image, so that it turns into a double-headed arrow.
- Click and drag to enlarge the image, so that it fills most of the page.
- When you are happy with the size, save and print. If the image quality is poor when enlarged, delete that image and find another.

How do I make a set of images to use on my interactive whiteboard?

There are plenty of tools either online or installed on your computer for compiling a folder of images to view. If you are unable to use online tools (such as Flickr), create a folder of the images that you want to use and then use the photo viewer or photo manager installed on your computer to view them as a slideshow (access the Help section if you are not sure how to do anything).

This guide assumes that you are using Microsoft Windows.

- Open Windows Explorer, create a new folder and place all the images that you want to use inside. You can use digital photos, jpegs, bitmaps, scans or any other common image file-type.
- Source any additional images you require from the internet and add to this folder.
- Open the folder and look for a link in the left-hand panel which says 'View as slideshow'. Click on this and the images will appear on the screen, one at a time, until you use the controls at the top to pause or exit the slideshow.

How can I find a sound-clip and play it through my classroom computer?

This guide assumes that you are using Microsoft Windows.

- Open a search engine and type 'free sound-clip' and whatever you are looking for, e.g. 'free sound-clip owls'.

- When you find a sound-clip that you like, save it as a .wav file (this will play in Windows Mediaplayer, which is installed on all computers using Microsoft Windows).
- Click on the file and it should automatically open and play in Windows Mediaplayer. If not, right-click on the file and select 'Open with . . .' and choose Windows Mediaplayer from the list of programs.
- Most sound-clips are very short, so to loop it right-click on the Microsoft button in the top left-hand corner of the player. Select 'play' from the menu, and then click 'repeat'. It will now play on a loop when you press play on the main controls.

NB: If you cannot hear the sound-clip, check that the volume control is not set on 'mute' by clicking on the speaker icon on the taskbar. (If you cannot see it but can see a little arrow head, click on the arrow to see the hidden icons.) Adjust the volume control. Close, and test your file again.

How do I create free email accounts online for topic characters/my class?

Before doing this, check with your ICT co-ordinator if email software has already been installed on your school computers that you could use.

- Go to a free email provider, such as Gmail, Yahoo or Hotmail. Follow the instructions to create an email account. When providing the username, make it relevant to your class, e.g. classfiveyeartwo, and choose a password that will be easy to remember, such as the class teacher's surname.
- Bear in mind that the fewer boxes you tick for bulletins and newsletters related to your class's interests, the less junk mail you will receive. If you can get away without ticking any, do so!
- Once you have created your class's account, open it, delete any welcome emails from the provider, and go to the Preferences tab. This will let you set the background colour to make it easier to read, and will also let you remove some other intrusive features such as newsfeeds. Save your changes.
- Now create another account for the topic characters who will be communicating with your class. Make the username relevant to the topic characters, as this will show up on all the emails that your class receive, e.g. islandquestkids. The password will not be used by the children so can be whatever is easy for you to remember.
- Set preferences as before and save any changes.

Spam and other unwanted emails

The best way to avoid spam finding its way into your class's email account is to avoid using the email address anywhere else on the internet.

Your email details may still be passed on to third parties by the service provider, however, so before using the email account with your class, always scan the list of unread emails and delete any that are irrelevant or inappropriate.

How can I make a voice recording on my computer?

This is a great trick to learn, and very simple. In my experience, even children in Year 5 can be foxed by their teacher speaking in a silly voice.

Most PCs and laptops have a straightforward recording device that picks up background noise as well as your voice, so try to find a quiet time for recording! If the sound quality is particularly bad, your ICT co-ordinator may have some microphones that you could use to improve the quality.

- If you have a Microsoft operating system, click on the Start button. Select All Programs, and look for the Sound Recorder in the main Accessories folder or in a sub-folder.
- To record yourself speaking, click the red Record button. When you have finished, click Stop.
- Save the file.
- If you are not happy with the recording when you play it back – possibly there is too much background noise, or you got your words in a tangle – just delete the file and start again.

Part 2: Links and further information

All of these web links were correct at the time of writing, but may have been altered since publication of this book.

First aid training

Although you will need any nominated first aider to have comprehensive and up-to-date training, it will do you no harm to brush up on your own first aid knowledge. The St John's Ambulance website has primers for cuts, fractures, shock and bleeding, a down-loadable first aid app for mobile phones, plus details of how to get further training.

http://www.sja.org.uk/sja/first-aid-advice.aspx

Specialised first aid training is available for working with young children in remote outdoor areas; try doing a web search using the term 'paediatric first aid outdoors'.

Forest School training

If you are interested in finding out more about the Forest Schools movement, including training opportunities near you, the Forestry Education Initiative website has a list of training providers. Each training organisation will have a slightly different take on the movement and its ethos, so try to get as much information as you can before booking and then choose the course that is the best fit for your interests.

http://www.foresteducation.org/woodland_learning/forest_schools/training_providers/

Learning Through Landscapes

The Learning Through Landscapes charity provides a wealth of useful information, including guides on how to adapt and enhance your school grounds for outdoor learning, training for teaching staff, teaching resources and ideas, and advice on corporate partnerships.

http://www.ltl.org.uk

Woodland Trust

This website is absolutely brilliant for outdoor learning ideas. Try looking at its seasonal activity guides, and check out the Nature Detectives section, which has full-colour, A4, printable identification guides for fauna and flora. You can use these activities with your class, or just enjoy them with your own children!

The Woodland Trust also has advice about planting trees and in the past has supplied trees to schools for free.

http://www.woodlandtrust.org.uk/en/Pages/default.aspx

Forestry Education Initiative (FEI)

The FEI provides information and teaching resources about trees, forests and products made from trees. It also has teaching resources and information about regional cluster groups for people who want to attend workshops and learn specific skills related to forestry or wood-related crafts, while providing networking opportunities with like-minded people.

http://www.foresteducation.org/

Forestry Commission

The Forestry Commission is the government department responsible for the management of Britain's woodlands. The Woodlands for Learning section of this website is divided into separate sections for England, Scotland and Wales, and provides a range of teaching resources and ideas.

http://www.forestry.gov.uk/website/fchomepages.nsf/hp/GBWFL

Federation of City Farms and Community Gardens

This website provides plenty of information about local organisations and projects that you might want to visit with your school, plus advice and contacts for the Growing Schools and Farm Schools initiatives.

http://www.farmgarden.org.uk/home

Equipment

Try doing your own search, or visit the following websites:

http://www.muddyfaces.co.uk – excellent prices for school budgets and prompt despatch.

http://www.forestschoolshop.co.uk – part of a larger company that also sells a wide range of bushcraft products.

Lottery funding

Awards for All provides Lottery-funded grants of up to £10,000 for community groups and projects, subject to the application meeting its regional outcome requirements.

http://www.awardsforall.org.uk

Community Assembly or local authority grants

At the time of writing, local authorities still have access to a supply of central government money for funding community projects. The amount can vary from £500 to £2,000. Contact your local authority and ask about the Community Assembly grants initiative, or any equivalent scheme for which you may be eligible.

Local industry and corporate volunteering

As part of their efforts to build strong links with the local community and maintain a positive reputation, many large businesses provide funding and manpower for improvement works in school grounds and community spaces. Insurance companies, banks and local industries have all participated. Scan local papers for publicity about recent charitable works and contact the company involved, or search the internet for current initiatives.

Appendix 1: Risk assessment grid

1. Use, add to or remove the risks listed below, as appropriate for your setting.
2. Then score the Probability of each risk from 1 to 5 (1 being very unlikely, 5 being unavoidable) and the Severity (1 not serious to 5 very serious).
3. Now multiply the Probability score for each risk with its Severity score (P × S), e.g. Probability of 2 × Severity of 3 = 6. Any risk with a P × S score of 12 or above must be dealt with immediately. Note any actions on your risk assessment grid, and tick them off once completed.

Name of school:... **Date:**....................

Name of teacher:... **Area of school grounds:** ....

Section	Risk	Harm	Probability	Severity	P × S	Mitigation/by whom	Done
Site preparation	Touching broken glass or rusted metal	Cuts, infection				Litter pick by teacher prior to session.	
	Touching stinging nettles or bramble thorns	Rash or scratches				Clear the site of any growth that will hinder the children's access. Show children which plants to avoid touching.	
Moving around site	Tripping over on uneven ground	Bruises, sprains				Children to conduct risk assessment of site with teacher prior to use. Teacher to remind of risks.	
	Bumping into tree/ each other	Bruises, concussion				Teacher to remind children to move safely around site at all times, and enforce rules.	
	Dragging sticks and other materials	Facial injury, scratches				Teacher to show children how to drag materials along the ground so as to avoid facial injuries.	
Canopy	Low-hanging dead branch, ready to fall out of tree	Head injury, concussion				Teacher to inspect site and try to pull down any hanging dead wood prior to session.	
	Low branches	Concussion, bruising				Teacher to note locations of low branches with children, and tie crepe strip around tip to ensure that they can be seen.	

Section	Risk	Harm	Probability	Severity	P × S	Mitigation/by whom	Done
	Twigs at eye level	Facial injury, scratches				As above.	
Scrub	Stinging nettles/ brambles	Rash or scratches				Clear the site of any growth that will hinder the children's access. Show children which plants to avoid touching.	
	Insects pollinating flowers	Bee sting/allergic reaction to insect bite				Teacher to be aware of locations of flowering plants and remind the children to be careful. Teacher to check medical notes for any children who have allergic reaction to insect bites and stings.	
Ground	Surface litter	Scratches, transfer of bacteria				Teacher to remove any visible litter prior to session.	
	Protruding roots/tree stump	Trips, slips and bruises				Teacher and children to note location of roots/tree stumps and to move around the site carefully.	
	Buried litter, including broken glass or rusty metal	Scratches, infection				Teacher to inspect site for protruding, sharp litter and remove, where possible. Where not possible, teacher to advise children of location so that they can avoid it.	
Hygiene	Dirty hands from handling soil and natural materials	Stomach upsets, feeling ill				No food or drink to be consumed during activities. Children reminded by teacher to wash hands thoroughly upon return to school building.	

Section	Risk	Harm	Probability	Severity	P × S	Mitigation/by whom	Done
Injury and illness	Child X needs to use epipen	Fit, unconsciousness				Teacher to check medical records for children who have an epipen at school, familiarise themselves with its use, and be aware of health condition it has been prescribed for. Teacher to note storage location of epipen.	
	Child X needs to use inhaler	Asthma attack, breathing difficulties				Teacher to check medical records for children who have an inhaler at school, familiarise themselves with its use, and be aware of health condition it has been prescribed for. Teacher to note storage location of inhaler. See also: 'Moving around site', page 128.	

Appendix T1L1

Dear children,

Our names are Carrie and Farid and we are lost in an enchanted forest. We're writing to you because we need your help to get home! Luckily, we met a talking owl who said he would help us. He delivered this letter to your classroom when no one would see.

There are lots of things about being in an enchanted forest that are great; all the birds and animals can talk, and there is an incredible stream with water that tastes of lemonade! Plus our friend the owl says he will speak to the Wizard of the Misty Mountain and see if he knows of any spells to help us get home.

It's very cold at night though, and we have to climb up a tree to sleep so the bears can't find us. It's very uncomfortable and sometimes we worry that we'll hurt ourselves. We desperately need somewhere cosy and comfortable to sleep, built out of the kinds of things we can find here: sticks, twigs, leaves and so on. We've never made anything like this before, so we don't really know where to start.

Can you try building some mini-shelters and then send us your ideas?

Thanks,

Carrie and Farid

Appendix T1L2

Dear children,

Wow, what a lot of brilliant ideas! We have used them to build a really cosy shelter, with soft beds made from bracken and dried leaves, and a bench made from a tree stump that we rolled up against the wall.

Now, here's our next problem. Do you remember that we mentioned the bears? Well, it turns out that they're not interested in eating us after all, but they are very interested in stealing our food! Last night they found our food bag and they have eaten everything, including the bag! We urgently need to make a special hiding place for our food supplies. We know that the bears can't see very well, because they depend on their sense of smell to find food. Maybe we could hang it from a tree, or bury it underground . . . or create some kind of camouflaged hiding place?

As you can see, we have lots of ideas and not much time to try them all out. Can you help?

Thanks,

Carrie and Farid

Appendix T1L3

Dear children,

Thanks for your ideas about hiding our food supply. The bears haven't found it since!

Since then we have found a patch of wild strawberries, and a talking squirrel told us where to find fresh hazelnuts. We picked as many as we could carry, and then left the path to find the enchanted stream. We ate them sitting on the bank in the sun, and then waded in to wash them down with great big gulps of lemonade.

We fell asleep under a tree and when we woke up it was getting dark. We couldn't remember how to get back to the shelter, as we'd left the path. All the trees looked the same in the shadows. We were wandering around for what felt like hours in the darkness before we finally found our way home.

What can we do to avoid losing our way next time? We thought of Hansel and Gretel dropping breadcrumbs, but of course the birds ate those. Do you think stones would work? Sticks? How about unwinding a really long piece of string? Or perhaps we should make some kind of map? We don't want the path to look very obvious, in case a hungry animal follows us.

Thanks,

Carrie and Farid

Appendix T1L4

Dear children,

We're pleased to report that since we last heard from you, we haven't got lost again! Who would have thought that such simple ideas could work so well? Thanks for trying those out for us.

Now, we have some pretty exciting news to share. Do you remember we mentioned a Wizard who might know a spell to help us home? Well, he told the owl that he had found all the ingredients and will meet us by a heart-shaped lake at the top of the Misty Mountain.

The only problem is that two giant, scaly, fire-breathing dragons make their nests in the peaks of the Misty Mountain. The owl told us that their sense of smell is very poor because their nostrils are scorched, but their eyesight is sharper than an eagle's. We will have to camouflage ourselves so that the dragons can't spot us when they are circling lazily in the skies above the mountain. We will be walking along a woodland path. Can you help us to design camouflage hats to wear? We're quite nervous about getting it wrong and would appreciate your ideas.

Thanks,

Carrie and Farid

Appendix T1L5

Dear children,

With any luck this is the last letter we'll have to write to you all! Thanks so much for your camouflage ideas; we managed to creep past those evil dragons without them noticing, although we were both quite scared. Since you last heard from us, we have met the Wizard by the heart-shaped lake, and he has cast a spell that will send us home in two days' time. We are waiting in a cave in the side of the Misty Mountain for the next full moon, when it will work. We are hidden from the dragons here and we even have some food to keep us going.

As you can imagine, we're really happy to be going home, but we're also . . . well . . . quite bored! We can't leave the cave for two days, and we're running out of jokes to tell each other. As one last favour, do you think that you could write us a story to read? We absolutely love stories, especially exciting ones about people having adventures. We would love to while away our last few days here reading your stories about some children lost in a strange forest.

Thanks again for your help and support. We couldn't have done it without you!

Your friends,

Carrie and Farid

Appendix T2C1

Forest club: Chapter 1

The four children paused to draw their breath. One held her sides, another panted and leant against a tree.

"This is perfect for Forest Club!" a boy called Josh declared.

"What's Forest Club?" gasped another girl called Shannon, who had flung herself onto the ground.

"*This* is Forest Club," Josh replied. "Here." He waved his arm around the clearing in the woods where they had been playing chase.

The other boy, Finn, threw himself down next to Shannon. "Yeah, that's what we'll call it. When we come here to play."

"And we've got the rest of the holidays to come!" enthused Farzana. She pulled a leaf out of her hair. "Forest Club is the best place for hide and seek."

"And we can have our sandwiches sitting on those logs," added Finn, gesturing towards a small clearing.

They sat silently for a while, watching the pattern of the sky through the leaves. It was Josh who broke the silence.

"D'you think that anyone else comes here?" he asked.

"What – people or animals?" replied Finn. They were all quiet for a moment, and then Shannon said, "Wait! I can hear something now! There, up in the tree!"

They all looked at where she was pointing, but couldn't see anything. Then a tinkling birdsong spilled out from the tree-top.

"What bird is that?" whispered Farzana. "It's not a cuckoo, is it?"

"A cuckoo? Why?" asked Shannon.

"Because I heard that they steal other birds' nests. Honestly! They push out the little birds and then lay their own eggs there."

No one was sure whether that was true, but no one liked the idea that it might be. It was Shannon who got up first. "Well, I'm going to make a spare nest, then," she decided.

"A spare nest?" scoffed Finn. "Out of what, exactly?"

"Twigs! Leaves. Moss. Er . . ."

"Grass," added Josh. "Feathers. Good idea, I'm making one too."

And so it was that, at Forest Club that day, the children all found themselves carefully winding and weaving together the materials for their nests, placing the nests carefully between branches or inside bushes, and decorating them with special things.

Appendix T2C2

Forest club: Chapter 2

They had spent the morning building dens, and were now sitting in the clearing eating their sandwiches. As usual, Josh wolfed his food down and then disappeared to find sticks.

Farzana picked at her lunch and pushed the rest away. "Not hungry today," she declared, and put it back in her bag. "I'm going to go and find something interesting."

Shannon and Finn exchanged looks, and carried on eating.

Five minutes later, Farzana crashed back triumphantly into the clearing. "Look!" she said, holding something on her outstretched hand.

Shannon put her lunch box back in her rucksack and glanced over. "What is it?"

Farzana was grinning mischievously. "Can't you tell?"

By now, Finn was looking at it too. "Bring it over, so we can see it better," he requested.

Obligingly, Farzana pushed her hand right into his face.

"Whoa!" he said, backing away and rubbing his eyes. He reached out and touched it, and then shook his head. "Er, Farzana? I thought you said you were going to find something interesting. This is a *twig*."

Shannon hooted appreciatively. "Farzana, are you mad? There must be *millions* of twigs out here!"

Farzana seemed unperturbed. "No, this isn't a twig. It's . . .," she paused for dramatic effect. "It's . . . an owl's walking stick. He dropped it from the trees when he was startled by a strange noise last night."

Josh appeared by her side. "I thought that it was a gymnastics beam for mice to practise their balancing on."

In response to Shannon's sceptical look, he continued: "Haven't you heard of mice doing beam work in gym? They just find a couple of stones, roll them into position, place the stick from end to end and then – tadah! – they can do this . . ." and he jumped on a log and pranced across it in an exaggerated manner.

"See?" concluded Farzana. "It's *not* a stick. I've rethought it."

After that, I'm sure you can imagine that the children spent a good while finding and rethinking things. Acorns became bowling balls for crows. Leaves became doormats for spiders. But then Shannon called them over. "Look at this and tell me what it is," she said, holding something strange on her palm.

It seemed to be a leaf, with a small twig rising up out of it. That twig also had a leaf threaded onto it, through two holes made by Shannon's fingers. It almost looked like a sail, made from a leaf. Suddenly Finn had an idea.

"It's a boat for getting across big puddles!"

Shannon beamed. "Who for?" she quizzed.

"A shrew, of course," replied Josh, as though it were a silly question. "I'm going to make one for a blackbird." And so off they went, to build their puddle-boats.

Appendix T2C3

Forest club: Chapter 3

It had been Finn's idea for them all to flop on their backs and stare up at the tree tops. So that's why, ten minutes later, they were still lying there with the dappled sunlight falling on their faces and a soft breeze brushing their cheeks.

Typically enough, it was Farzana who broke the silence.

"Giant," she murmured.

"Eh?" Josh tilted his head towards her. "What are you talking about?"

Farzana gestured upwards, to the soaring trees. "Them."

Giant, thought Shannon. And then an even better word popped into her head. "Statuesque!" she declared, even surprising herself.

This time they all tilted their heads towards her. "Statuesque?" repeated Finn, carefully. "What on earth does that mean?"

"Like a statue! Huge, impressive, still." Josh shrugged dismissively – which was quite hard to do when he was lying on his back – and turned away again.

But Shannon was enthused. "Finn, what do you think?"

Finn scrunched up his eyes, which meant that he was thinking, and then said, in a tiny little voice: "Whispering."

Both girls burst out laughing in agreement. "It's true! The leaves are whispering."

"And sighing," added Josh, who seemed to have joined in the game. "Like their branches are aching from holding up all those leaves and birds' nests." He stood up, dusting himself down.

"Where are you going?" asked Shannon.

"Going to make myself a tree."

"Make yourself a tree? But there's plenty of real ones, here."

"Yeah, I know. But . . ." He paused. "I want to take one home with me."

Shannon understood. Josh lived in a third floor flat, so he didn't have a garden. And the only trees in the recreation ground by his house weren't really trees at all; they were stubby, and bush like, and sometimes had rubbish stuck in them.

Finn had propped himself up on his elbow, suddenly interested.

"How are you going to do it?"

Josh didn't say anything, and for a moment it felt as though he didn't really know.

But then Farzana started rifling through her rucksack. With a slap, she threw her pencil case on the soil, quickly followed by her notebook.

"Collage," she answered.

As Josh threw her a grateful glance, she unzipped her pencil case and continued: "We'll make a collage of a tree, using bits of what we can find out here. And we'll stick it all down with this!"

And then she threw a glue stick at Finn, which narrowly missed his head.

So Josh got to take his tree home after all.

Appendix T2C4

Forest club: Chapter 4

That morning, they arrived at Forest Club with no particular plans. Shannon had gone to find her special stick and had then gone off, looking for interesting things. Farzana had sat still for a while, listening to the birdsong and thinking about all the different kinds of green there were in the woods. The boys had gone off to find some large stones, which they would put to use when they had thought of something to build with them.

After a little while, Shannon came and sat down next to Farzana. She put down her stick, and then reached carefully into her pockets.

"Found some treasure?" enquired Farzana, as Shannon emptied out her booty, nodding.

"Cool!" The other girl held out her hands for Shannon to fill, and then they spread her finds on the ground: a delicate purple flower, some red-coloured foil, a small stone with a hole in it and a long piece of grass with a tuft at the top.

"What are all these for?" asked Farzana.

Shannon smiled, and took her stick. "For decorating this." She pulled some sellotape from her rucksack and tore a piece off. "To make it look nice."

"Yeah, I can see that," agreed Farzana. Shannon carefully picked up the purple flower, and placed it against the bark. "Is this a violet?" she asked, but Farzana was off in her own world.

"Violet . . . Violet, princess of the woodland," she murmured, "was the king's only daughter."

Shannon smiled and reached for the piece of grass, which she started to wind around her stick.

"One day," Farzana continued, "Princess Violet was walking through a field of grass when a wicked witch cast a spell to make it suddenly grow high and tangle her up so she couldn't escape . . ."

Shannon had by now picked up the red-coloured foil.

"And so she was locked in a dungeon, but a passing prince saw her ruby ring glinting in the dark and knew something was wrong. He resolved to pass by again the following night. So . . ."

Farzana paused, watching Shannon's hands to see what she picked up next. She went for the stone with a hole in.

"So Princess Violet used the spoon she was given to eat her gruel to dig a hole out of her dungeon. She dug a tunnel which took her out. When she burst through to escape she was exhausted and dying of thirst, but luckily the prince was waiting and gave her some water."

Shannon gave a round of applause, waving her decorated stick in the air. "Brilliant! So what do you call that, then?"

Finn, who had by now come over to listen with Josh, said: "A story stick."

"Let's make one!" cried Josh, running off into the trees to find things for theirs.

Appendix T2C5

Forest club: Chapter 5

It was the last day of the holidays, and so the last visit to Forest Club. Next week, they would all be back at school, with a new teacher. So as they trooped across the field and into the trees that hid their playing place, they were all thinking of what they would like to do.

I'd like to climb that big oak tree, thought Shannon. *I'm going to finish inventing my stick-throwing game*, thought Finn. But Farzana didn't have a chance to finish her thoughts, because they were all alerted by a sudden cry. Something was wrong!

They rushed to the clearing, where Josh was standing, gesturing at a huge pile of branches and sticks. It took them a moment to remember that yesterday that huge pile had been a den that they had spent all day building. Why was it all lying on the ground, like rubble? Their minds swam. A crisp packet blew past in the breeze, and Finn's eye fell on a drink can. *Teenagers!* he thought.

"Some teenagers have destroyed our den," he said grimly. "Look – there's a drink can that one of them must have left. And an empty packet of crisps. *Typical.*"

The others were quiet, thinking. Shannon retrieved the can and looked at it. Its label was so faded that it was hard to tell what drink it had contained.

"But this can is so old it can't have been dropped yesterday. Maybe it's been here all along and we never noticed it." She picked up the crisp packet. "And this could have just blown in from the field."

"Fair enough," said Josh, "but it still doesn't explain why our den has collapsed." They looked at it sadly.

"Maybe some animals had a scuffle and knocked it down," ventured Farzana. She kicked the ground with her shoe. "Look – scuff marks." Sure enough, the soil by the side of the den was bumpy and rough looking, as though some sort of scuffle had taken place. And was that a necklace lying in the dirt? "Or maybe some robbers were hiding here from the police."

"Or maybe a really huge owl landed on top and made it collapse," offered Finn, breaking the sombre atmosphere by making the others laugh.

"Who knows?" replied Shannon, moving forward. "But I think we should rebuild it anyway. And while we're doing it, we can make up a story about the mysterious events of last night."

Appendix T2L1

Gnarled	Green	Stretching
Ancient	Giant	Sheltering
Tall	Whispering	Wide
Mysterious	Rustling	Tranquil
Wise	Friendly	Rough
Aged	Smooth	Red
Beautiful	Changing	Orange
Graceful	Growing	
Magnificent	Trembling	

Appendix T3J1

General facts

Dark, shaggy fur with a white furry belly	Red-brown coloured eyes	Wolf-like shape
Large, pointed ears like a fox	Shelters in a burrow from the daytime heat	Eats small parrots and tree frogs

Appendix T3J2

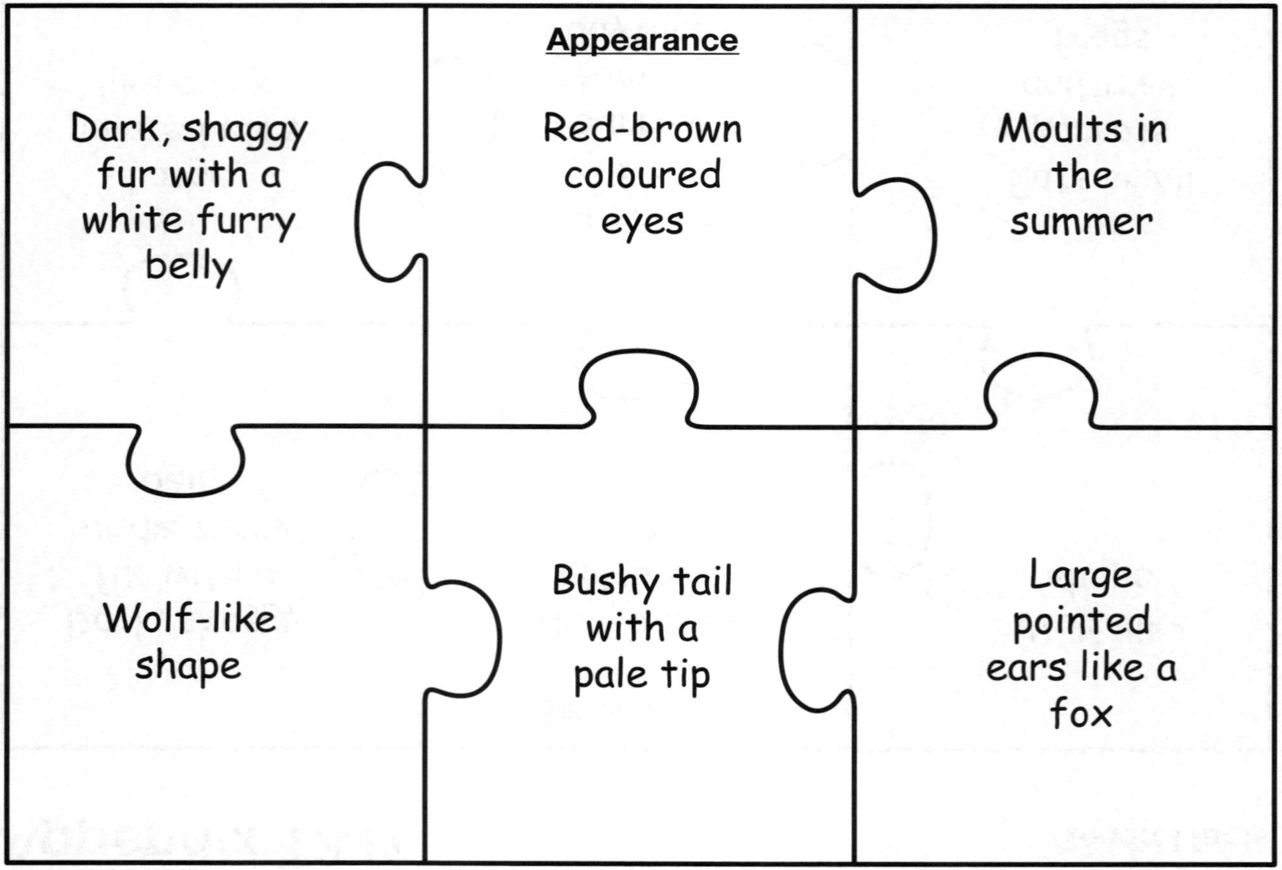
Appearance
Dark, shaggy fur with a white furry belly
Red-brown coloured eyes
Moults in the summer
Wolf-like shape
Bushy tail with a pale tip
Large pointed ears like a fox

Appendix T3J3

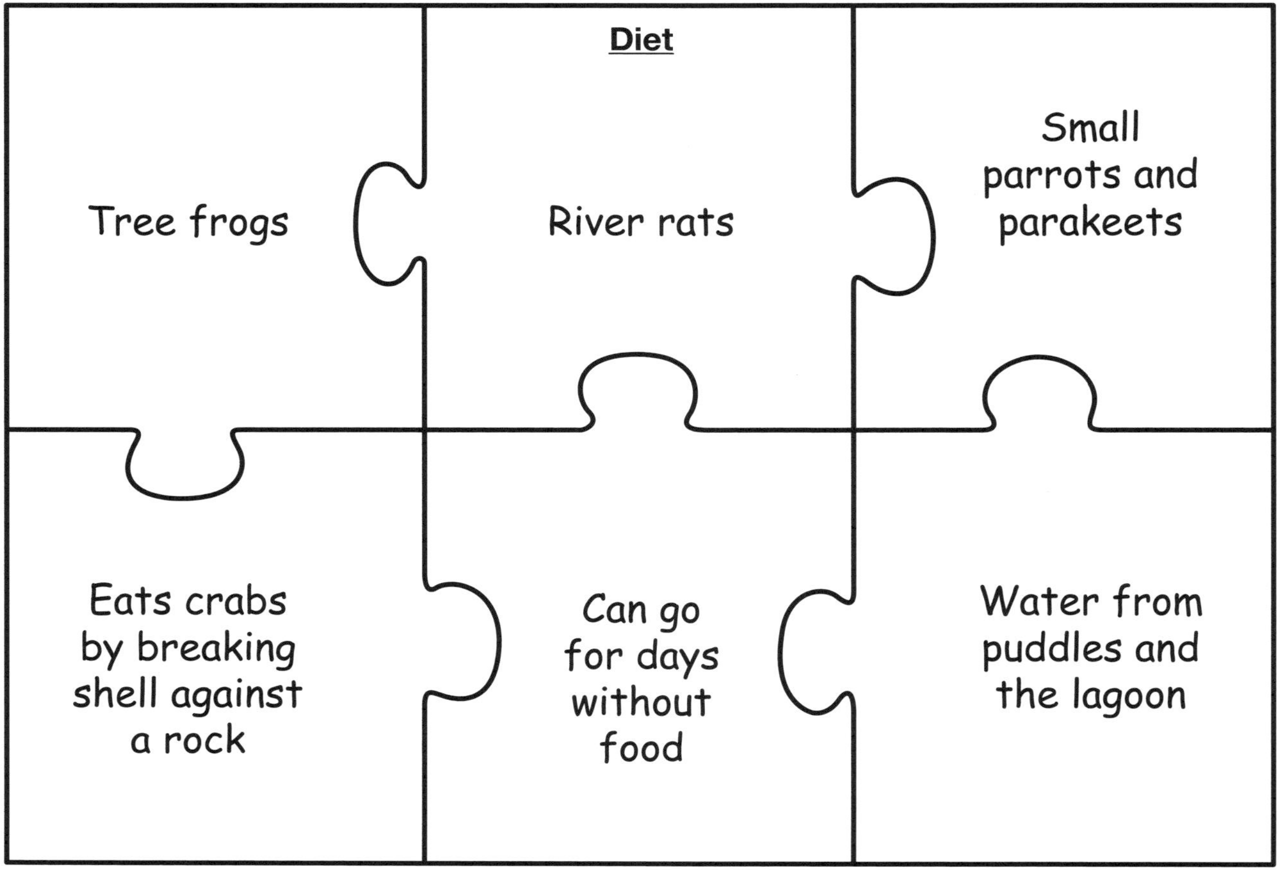
Diet
Tree frogs
River rats
Small parrots and parakeets
Eats crabs by breaking shell against a rock
Can go for days without food
Water from puddles and the lagoon

Appendix T3J4

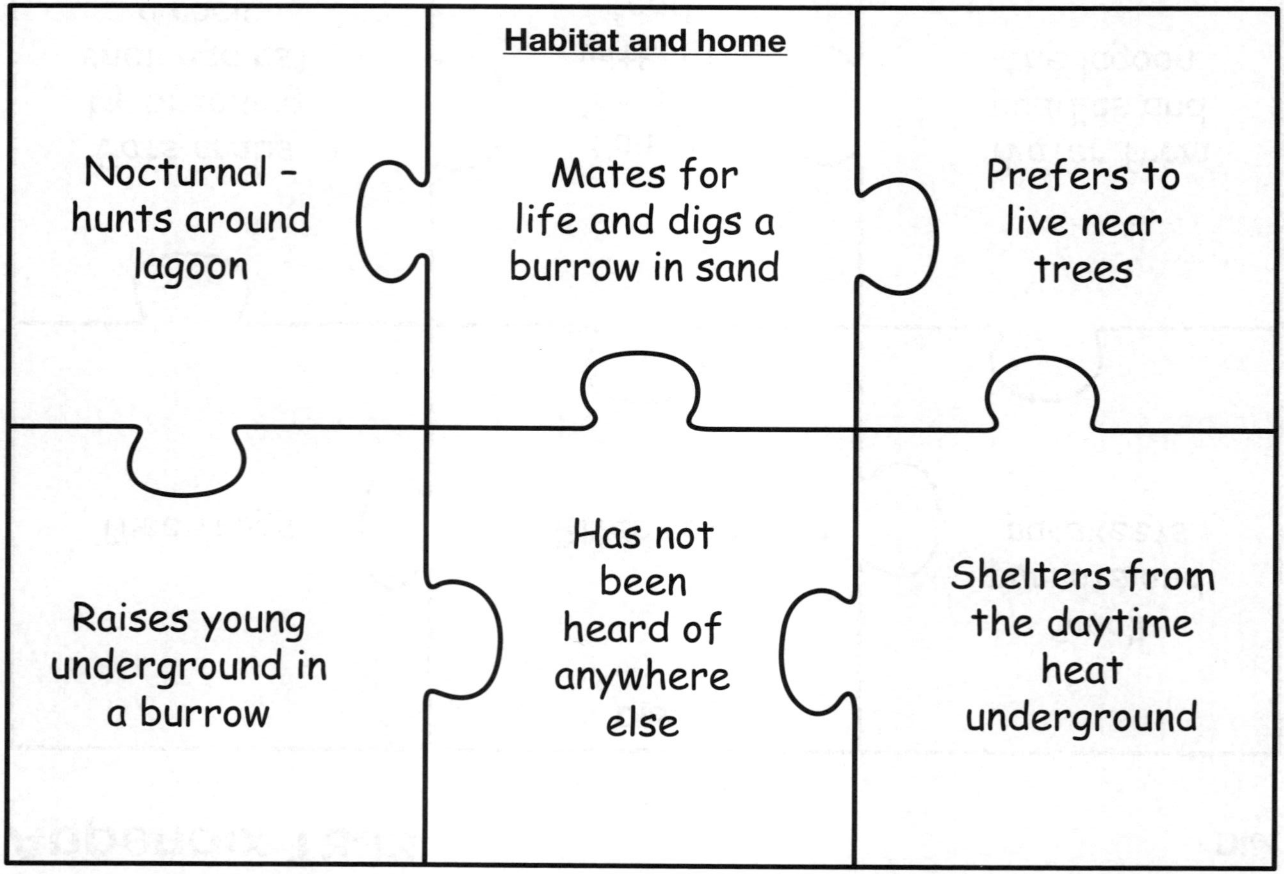
Habitat and home
Nocturnal - hunts around lagoon
Mates for life and digs a burrow in sand
Prefers to live near trees
Raises young underground in a burrow
Has not been heard of anywhere else
Shelters from the daytime heat underground

Appendix T3J5

Other interesting facts

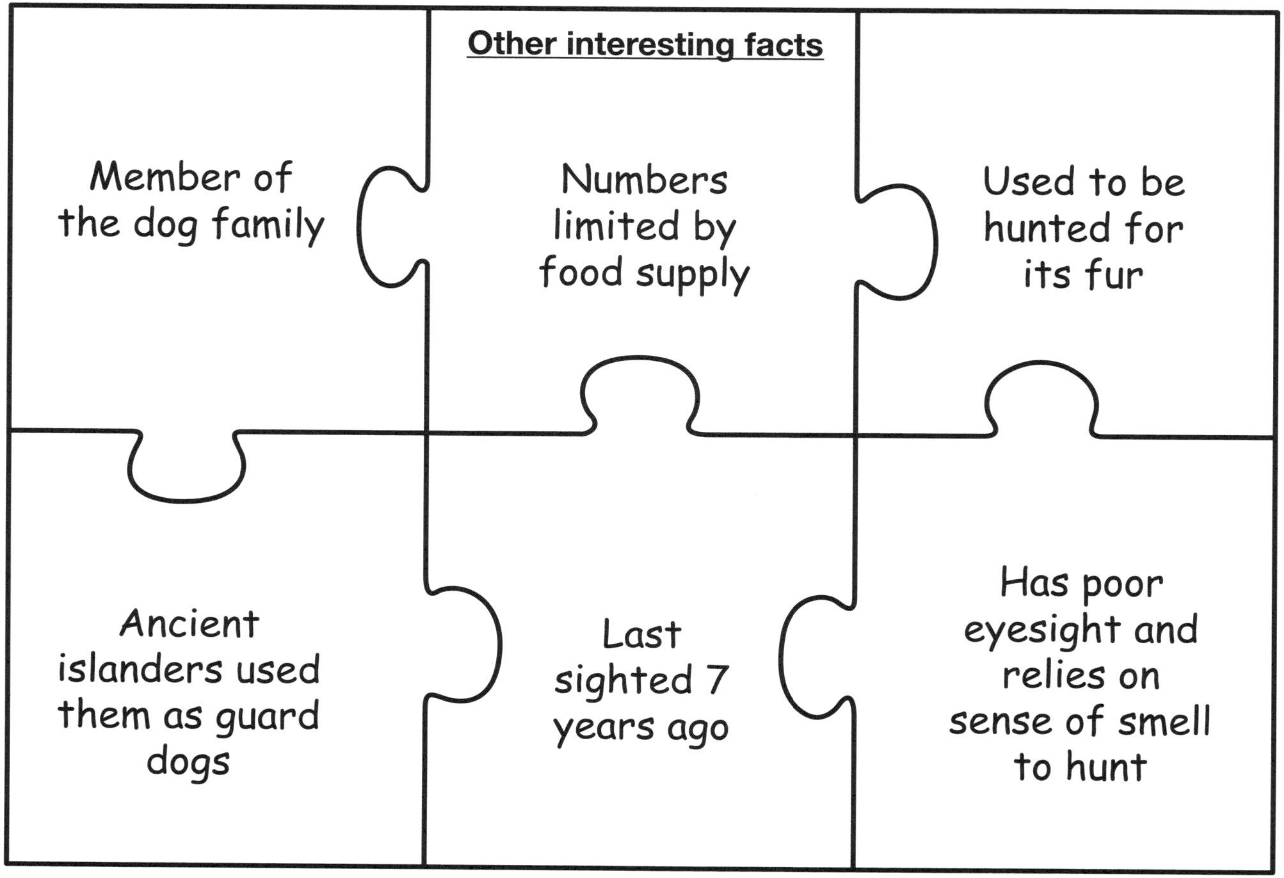
Other interesting facts
Member of the dog family
Numbers limited by food supply
Used to be hunted for its fur
Ancient islanders used them as guard dogs
Last sighted 7 years ago
Has poor eyesight and relies on sense of smell to hunt

Appendix T3L1

Hello!

We expect you're wondering who on earth we are, so here goes! Our names are Ty, Connie, Joe and Sammy . . . and we're on a special mission to investigate the moon-beast.

Have you ever heard of the moon-beast before? It's rumoured to live on an island off the coast of Japan. We're volunteers for an international wildlife charity, and have been sent here to find out whether it exists. We arrived on a motor-launch yesterday morning, just as the sun was rising over the tree-covered mountains and the parrots were beginning to squawk. We had all our gear in our backpacks, and jumped into the knee-deep waves to wade ashore. It felt like something out of a film! We have plenty of food supplies and a solar-powered laptop for keeping in touch with our friends on the mainland. But what we need some help with is protecting ourselves from the sun. We all got quite badly sunburned yesterday, and need to build some kind of sun-shelter that we can sit under when the sun is at its fiercest. We've got needles, thread, string and scissors, plus whatever we can lay our hands on here. We also found a stack of yellowed newspapers and empty sacks that must have been left by a fisherman.

If you could let us know your ideas, we'd be really grateful; the charity we work for thought your class would be good at this kind of thing so we can't wait to hear what you come up with!

Bye for now,

Connie, Ty, Joe and Sammy

Appendix T3L2

Hello again!

Thanks for all your ideas about building a sun-shelter.

As soon as we had read your emails we made two shelters, one for napping in the midday heat and one for relaxing in.

Since we last emailed you, we have made contact with the fisherman we mentioned last time. He didn't speak any English, but Ty is half Japanese so luckily he could talk to him about our mission. When he heard that we had come to investigate the moon-beast, he led us inland through a grove of palm trees and showed us a freshwater lagoon. He pointed to the tiny little islet in the middle, and Ty thought that he was telling us that we could find the moon-beast there. When Ty asked the fisherman how we could get across the water to the islet, he went very quiet and refused to answer. We thought we must have offended him, but eventually he told Ty that it might not be safe for us to go over there, and that he couldn't live with his conscience if anything happened to us. We all shook hands with him and thanked him for his help, and he took a good-luck charm from around his neck and gave it to Ty before leaving.

We can all swim, but we can't really tell how far away the islet is. The fisherman's boat is too big to drag through the trees, and anyway he wouldn't lend it to us if he knew where we wanted to go. Surely we could come up with some kind of raft? There's plenty of twine and string in our backpacks, and lots of logs and bamboo lying around. We've also got some empty water bottles if they're any use.

Could you come up with some prototype designs for us?

Thanks again,

Connie, Ty, Sammy and Joe

Appendix T3L3

Hello again!

Well, thanks for all your ideas for the raft. We managed to make one and took it in turns to row ourselves across, using a clipboard fastened to a bamboo cane as a paddle. We're all over here now on this tiny islet in the middle of the lagoon. No sign of the moon-beast yet, but we're being careful and going everywhere in pairs, just to be on the safe side. However, on the last journey across the lagoon, disaster struck!

Sammy was coming over on the last trip, and she had all of our notes and data about the moon-beast in a bundle, tied up with string. As she reached the shore of the islet, Joe ran forward to grab the front of the raft so she could climb off. No one really knows what happened next, but suddenly the raft tipped up, Sammy was soaked and the bundle of notes was sinking fast! Luckily Connie and Ty managed to fish them out and spread them out on the sand to dry. But that night the wind picked up while we were sleeping, and we woke up to find them all over the place – stuck up palm trees, trapped in bushes, or lying on the beach, half covered in sand.

We think we've gathered them all in again now, but they're in such a mess and very torn and disorganised. Can you help us to sort them out? We need to work out what we know about the moon-beast so far – especially now that we might be neighbours!

Thanks as ever,

Connie, Ty, Joe and Sammy

Appendix T3L4

Hey, it's us again!

Sorry to email you at such a strange time, but this is unbelievable. We think we might have found the moon-beast!

It's night-time here, and we were just packing up for bedtime when Connie heard a snuffling noise outside the tent. At first, she thought it was Ty being silly, but then it happened again just as Ty was denying it was him. We all went silent, looking at each other's faces. Then we heard it for a third time, and this time there was some scratching as well, like something was looking for food. Joe rolled his eyes and exclaimed, "Drat! We've left some of our food outside the tent – that's why the animals have found it. I'm going to go and collect it in, quickly – before even more turn up." Sammy grabbed a torch and said that she would go out too, and they left, zipping the mosquito net behind them. None of us was very worried, until we heard a sharp cry, and running footsteps. "We've seen it!" Sammy shouted. "It's out here, over by a rock!" So we grabbed our camera and dashed out, but then we heard some growling from the darkness behind the tent and we rushed back in, suddenly feeling quite unsafe.

"Send an email, quick – so that people know what's happening," said Connie, so that's what we're doing now.

Hang on a sec, what's that? We think we can hear voices in the undergrowth, and they're coming this w

Appendix T3L5

Hello again!

The first thing we want to say is that we're back on the mainland now, safe and sound. The second thing we want to say is how sorry we are about that worrying email we sent you! Some strange things happened that night and we had to leave the island in a hurry, but now we can explain what happened.

When we thought we had seen the moon-beast, we were right. What we didn't know was that the fisherman who told us where to find this strange creature had been very worried when he went home that day, and he had told his wife. She was terrified that something would happen to us, as we were going to visit the islet during a full moon. She made her husband go back to find us with one of his friends and take us off the islet! This is because, according to legend, the moon-beast becomes very territorial during the full moon and will attack anything that strays into its path. That's why we heard men's voices in the undergrowth, and why we had to leave so quickly.

But perhaps the strangest thing that has happened is that, since filing our report on the moon-beast, we have been approached by a film producer who thinks that our story would make a great movie! We're so busy catching up on schoolwork right now that we haven't had time to set our adventure down, but if you could help us we'd definitely include your names in the credits.

Thanks again for all your help,

Your friends Connie, Ty, Joe and Sammy

Appendix T4Cipher

This code substitutes each letter with a number, according to its position in the alphabet.

If you want to create a more challenging code for your class, try shifting the numbers along by 2, e.g. A=3, B=4.

Alternatively, give your class just enough time to figure out how the code works and then collect in the ciphers!

A	B	C	D	E	F	G	H	I	J	K	L	M	N	O	P	Q	R	S	T	U	V	W	X	Y	Z
1	2	3	4	5	6	7	8	9	10	11	12	13	14	15	16	17	18	19	20	21	22	23	24	25	26

Appendix T4E1

Eyewitness report by Reverend Grimsby

When?
Wednesday afternoon at the vicarage.
Who?
Two local handymen – I'm afraid I can't remember their names, but one was tall with black curly hair and the other was shorter, with a moustache.
What were they doing?
They had come to fix the gutter, which had got blocked with dead leaves and was leaking. They were very helpful at first, and very interested about the statues and silver candlesticks in the church. They asked me lots of questions about how much they were worth and whether they were antiques.
What did they say?
They had finished fixing the gutter and I had just paid them when the one with the moustache said, "Hey, hang on a minute – there's smoke coming from over there. Is your house on fire?" I rushed off to check, but the house was absolutely fine.
What happened next?
I was only away for a few minutes, but when I returned I couldn't find them. As I walked through the church looking for them, I noticed that some items had been stolen from the altar, including my spare white collar. I also found a strange bundle of folded up paper which I handed in to a police officer.

Appendix T4E2

Eyewitness report by Mrs Beattie

When?
Wednesday afternoon at the vicarage.
Who?
Two local handymen – one is called Plonk and the other one is known locally as Snifter. I'm afraid there are some rumours about them being criminals, but we believe in giving people a second chance at the church so the Reverend let them fix the guttering.
What were they doing?
They asked me lots of questions while I was polishing the candlesticks and cleaning down the statues on the altar. They wanted to know what time I finished working, and whether I left the doors to the church unlocked.
What did they say?
I was just about to lock up after finishing the cleaning when one of them said, "We're absolutely parched, could you go and make us a nice cup of tea?" It was just after the Reverend had paid them for their work, so I thought it was a bit odd that they wanted a cup of tea when they were about to go home.
What happened next?
I went to make them their drinks and then, when I returned, I found the Reverend pacing frantically about. I put the tray of tea down and glanced at the altar. That's when I realised that things were missing. "We've been robbed!" said the Reverend. He looked very worried. We called the police immediately. I also noticed that some of my cleaning things were missing.

Appendix T4F1

Fact file: HIGHLY CONFIDENTIAL

Name:

13, 18, 19   2, 5, 1, 20, 20, 9, 5

Appearance:

15, 12, 4   12, 1, 4, 25

Job:

3, 8, 21, 18, 3, 8   3, 12, 5, 1, 14, 5, 18

Other information:

12, 9, 11, 5, 19   7, 1, 18, 4, 5, 14, 9, 14, 7

Appendix T4F2

Fact file: HIGHLY CONFIDENTIAL

Name:

18, 5, 22, 5, 18, 5, 14, 4   7, 18, 9, 13, 19, 2, 25

Appearance:

15, 12, 4

23, 5, 1, 18, 19   1   23, 8, 9, 20, 5   3, 15, 12, 12, 1, 18

Job:

22, 9, 3, 1, 18

Other information:

3, 15, 12, 12, 5, 3, 20, 19   1, 14, 20, 9, 17, 21, 5, 19

Appendix T4F3

Fact file: HIGHLY CONFIDENTIAL

Name:

18, 15, 14   16, 12, 15, 14, 11

Appearance:

20, 1, 12, 12

2, 12, 1, 3, 11   8, 1, 9, 18

Job:

8, 1, 14, 4, 25, 13, 1, 14

Other information:

16, 12, 1, 25, 19   6, 15, 15, 20, 2, 1, 12, 12

Appendix T4F4

Fact file: HIGHLY CONFIDENTIAL

Name:

1, 18, 3, 8, 9, 5   19, 14, 9, 6, 20, 5, 18

Appearance:

19, 8, 15, 18, 20

13, 15, 21, 19, 20, 1, 3, 8, 5

Job:

8, 1, 14, 4, 25, 13, 1, 14

Other information:

12, 9, 11, 5, 19   4, 15, 7, 19

Appendix T4F5

Full name	**Ronald Plonk**
Age	**47 years old**
Height	**Tall**
Hair	**Black and curly**
Job	**Handyman**
Hobbies	**Plays football – was goalie for team while in prison**
Previous convictions	**Robbery**
Distinguishing marks	**A scar down one arm from falling off a ladder while breaking into a house**

Appendix T4F6

Full name	Archie Snifter
Age	52 years old
Height	Short
Hair	Short and brown
Job	Handyman
Hobbies	Trains dogs to bark in warning when the police approach
Previous convictions	Robbery
Distinguishing marks	A moustache, grown as a disguise for last robbery

Appendix T4L1

So you found our message, eh? Not bad for a bunch of kids.

Allow us to introduce ourselves. I'm Perks, and he's Malik. We're detectives. And right now we're investigating a burglary at St John's church which happened yesterday afternoon.

The reason we're contacting you is because you might be able to help us. We've received reports of suspicious behaviour on the night of the burglary in the school grounds. Eyewitnesses saw two people creeping about in the trees before being startled by a noise and running off. What we need to know is this: who were they?

There's two things we want you to do. First, comb the area for anything which the intruders might have dropped. Then take a look at the files we have on the four people who are currently suspects, and decide which two fit the bill. Oh by the way, the files are strictly confidential, so they're written in code. But we've given you a cipher to crack it with, so you clever kids shouldn't have any problem with that.

OK? Good luck!

Detectives Martha Perks and Zac Malik

Appendix T4L2

Perks and Malik here.

OK, so we've read your letters. Our first thought was: the cleaning lady and the Reverend Grimsby? Are you *sure*? But we admit that the evidence you found does seem to point to them.

Now we've got something else for you to look at. A mysterious bundle was found by the entrance to the church, and it seems to contain some coded information, local maps and pictures. We haven't had time to take a proper look, but we'd like you to work out what it is. We've made some copies and hidden them in a safe place for you to find. We've also put the cipher in there.

Good luck code-breaking – we look forward to finding out what it all means!

Detectives Perks and Malik

Appendix T4L3

Hi. Perks and Malik here.

You did a good job on decoding that package. As soon as we had read your messages, we checked the time and raced around to St Aidan's church to warn the vicar that his church was going to be targeted.

Unfortunately we were too late to stop the burglary; as we pulled up outside we saw two people running off, with what looked like quite a large bag. But this is the strange thing: our two prime suspects, Mrs Beattie and the Reverend Grimsby, were busy at their church hosting a Women's Institute meeting. So we know that they didn't burgle St Aidan's church. And here's another thing: on the day that St John's church was burgled, some workmen had been around to fix the guttering. Those workmen were Ron Plonk and Archie Snifter, two of our original suspects.

Can you make some 'Wanted!' posters for us with detailed descriptions of the suspects? We've left what information we have about them in the woods. And keep an eye on those school grounds of yours – perhaps they'll turn up again.

Thanks for your help,

Detectives Perks and Malik

Appendix T4L4

Hi kids,

This is a pretty short letter today to say that we intercepted a coded message between Plonk and Snifter, and we think that the dastardly pair will turn up anytime now to hide their stolen goods.

Take good care of yourselves and let us know if you see or hear anything suspicious. We'll need as much detail as possible. What the suspects were wearing, anything they did or said, and anything that you found in the area. We think we're close to solving this one!

Detectives Perks and Malik

Appendix T4L5

Well, goodness me. Talk about lucky timing!

Thanks to your eyewitness reports, we have been able to catch Ronald Plonk and Archie Snifter. They should be in court right now and will soon be behind bars. We have also been able to return all those stolen goods.

We thought you'd be interested to hear Plonk and Snifter's side of the story, now that they have confessed to the burglaries. They were fixing the gutter at the Reverend Grimsby's church when they noticed that the church was empty, and went in to find valuable things to steal. They were startled on the way out by a visitor, and in the panic to hide the stolen goods in a sack, they picked up Mrs Beattie's cleaning things and the Reverend Grimsby's spare collar and Bible. They also dropped their secret plans for robbing St Aidan's.

They then waited until nightfall and climbed into the school grounds to hide while they sorted out their booty, throwing away the things that they thought were worthless.

They had us all fooled for a while that poor Mrs Beattie and Reverend Grimsby were the burglars, but luckily you set us straight. Now we want you to do one more thing: can you write a full account of what happened for our crime report? We can then close the case.

Thanks again for all your help,

Detectives Perks and Malik

Appendix T4List

Where:

19, 20. 1, 9, 4, 1, 14, 19 3, 8, 21, 18, 3, 8

Equipment:

12, 1, 4, 4, 5, 18

20, 15, 18, 3, 8

19, 1, 3, 11

Steal:

7, 15, 12, 4 19, 20, 1, 20, 21, 5

2, 25 20, 8, 5 1, 12, 20, 1, 18

Appendix T4Map

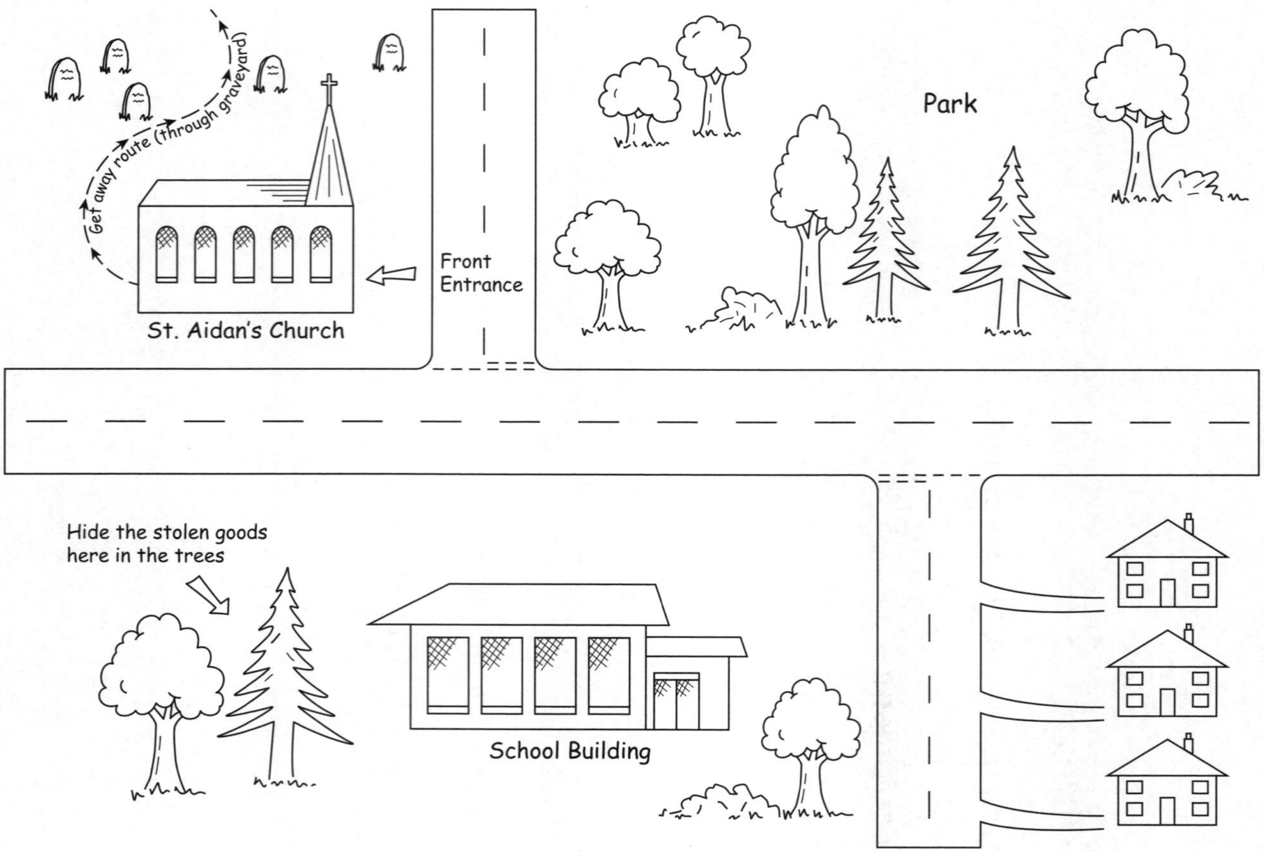

Park
Front
Entrance
Get away route (through graveyard)
St. Aidan's Church
Hide the stolen goods
here in the trees
School Building

Appendix T4W1

Eyewitness report

When?
Who?
What were they doing?
What did they say?
What happened next?

Appendix T4W2

Detective's name
Date and time
Location
Protagonists
Alleged crime
Crime description

Appendix T4W3

Detective's name
Place of the crime
Who did it?
What did they do?
How did they do it?

Appendix T5L1

Greetings to you!

Our names are Caedmon and Brina, and we are two children from the Iceni tribe. Caedmon means 'wise warrior' and Brina means 'protector'. We used to live a proud and brave life in a Welsh hill-fort, but sadly our tribe died many years ago.

A wise druid has helped us to find a way to travel through time, and we have a special mission we must complete for our people. You might have heard of the Iceni, and you might even have heard of hill-forts. But do you know what these looked like? Have you ever seen an Iceni warrior painting his or her face for battle? Have you smelled the stew bubbling in an iron cauldron over a wood fire in the roundhouse? Have you touched the cloth woven on looms by our craftswomen to make our clothes? Of course not, because much of our history has been lost over time; the wood, straw, fabric and leather of our lives has rotted in the earth where it was buried. But we have come to show you what it was like to be a Celt, and to think and live as we did.

The first thing we would like to show you is how we built our houses. They were round, with low walls made of wattle and daub, and high, pointed roofs made from straw. Do you know what wattle and daub is? The wattle is sticks and branches woven together, and the daub is a mixture of animal dung, mud, clay and water. It's very sticky and blocks out the wind and rain when you smear it thickly over the wattle! You might want to just use mud and clay though . . . it can be a bit smelly.

May the gods protect you,

Caedmon and Brina

Appendix T5L2

Goodness, what amazing roundhouses! Habondia, our goddess of hearth and home, would be proud.

Do you know how important the gods and goddesses were to us? We lived in a time long ago, before the invention of electric light and heat, and we had not heard of science. We thought that all natural forces were gods and goddesses; the wind, the sun, the water and so on. If you spent a night on a wind-swept hill-fort in the pitch-black night, watching the flames of the fire dance and glow, perhaps you could begin to understand why we felt that way.

We used to sing songs and tell stories to remember our gods and goddesses, and there were hundreds of them. Sabrina was the water goddess, Taramis was the god of the sky, and Cernunos was the god of the harvest. We also had gods of war, of course, as Celtic tribes were often at war with one another.

Both men and women would fight to protect their homes – hence the meaning of our names – and we would like you to join us in a ritual which brought us luck on the eve of war. We would make offerings to please the gods by throwing replica swords into a sacred river. We would decorate them beautifully in the hopes that the gods would like them and send us good luck to win the battle.

May the gods protect you,

Caedmon and Brina

Appendix T5L3

What a treasure trove of beautiful swords! It's almost a shame that you didn't have to charge into a bloodthirsty battle straight after making them; we're sure that the gods would have protected you well.

Of course, you might have already met one of our other friends. Look around you, very quietly. What was that movement in the trees? Listen, very carefully. Did you hear that twig crack? Look at the patterns in the leaves and the bark. Can you see him yet?

We're talking about the Green Man, of course. Do you know who he is? He is a mythical figure who appeared each spring, and disappeared at the end of each summer. Whenever the Green Man was around, the trees grew, the flowers bloomed and the fruit and vegetables grew. When he left, autumn and winter followed.

Celts weren't the only people to believe in the Green Man, and you can still find his face carved on the archways of old churches. His hair is often shown as leaves and he has a long beard. Can you make your own Green Man to bring springtime to your woods?

Caedmon and Brina

Appendix T5L4

Hello again friends,

We have one more thing to show you about our life and culture before we have to go home. Do you remember that we told you about our looms? We used them to make cloth from brightly coloured threads and wools.

Do you know how we made those bright colours? There was no such thing as paints or pens when we were alive, and so we had to make our own dyes from what we could find in the forest and the field. The Green Man was very important for making dyes, because we could only harvest the leaves, fruit, berries and flowers that we needed while he was around.

Making dyes was very simple; we collected up things that we thought had an interesting colour, and then we crushed them up with a smooth stone or a stick. Next we added some water and soil or chalk-dust to thicken the dye, and then we stirred in some animal urine to set the colour. That might not sound very nice today, but when we were alive we found a use for everything! This was because we had no factories to make things or shops to buy them in.

Today, you can try to make your dyes using the leaves, berries, fruit, soil and flowers around you. See what colours you can create.

May the gods protect you,

Caedmon and Brina

Appendix T5L5

Hello friends,

We hope that you enjoyed making your dyes last week. Sadly, the druid's magic is wearing off now, and so we have to travel back to our place of rest.

Do you remember that we said that we were children of the Iceni tribe? Our tribe was a fierce and proud one, and we were taught all the important skills of the day, but we never learned how to read or write. In fact, not even the druids learned how to read or write; they had to memorise all of their learning in stories and songs over many years.

We came to show you something about how we lived in Celtic times because the things we built and made had perished over thousands of years in the soil. But now that we have to leave, we are worried that this knowledge will rot in the same way. If we could write you a book of all we know we would, but we don't know how to. You can write, though. And you know other things about being a Celt that we haven't even had time to teach you. Would you write a book about Celtic life, so that other children might find out about us and understand us?

Your friends across time and history,

Caedmon and Brina

Appendix T6F1

Fact file: Grey squirrel

Eats acorns.
Builds a nest called a drey.
Lines its nest with moss in winter.
Eats tree buds, bark, leaves and fungi.
Lives in parks, cities and woodland.
Can leap and run along tree branches.
Lives for 3–4 years.
Uses its tail as a blanket while it sleeps.
Hides acorns in the ground for winter.
Has good eyesight.
Baby squirrels are blind until they are seven weeks old.

Appendix T6F2

Fact file: Song thrush

Has a speckled chest.
Kills and eats snails by smashing their shells against a stone.
Lives in woodland, parks and gardens.
Also eats worms and berries.
Song thrush eggs are blue with black spots.
Builds its nest in a bush or a tree.
Song thrushes know lots of different songs.
Has pink legs and a brown beak.
Farmers do not like song thrushes, as they eat their fruit crops.

Appendix T6F3

Fact file: Grey squirrel

Eats acorns.
Builds a nest the size of a football called a drey.
Lines its drey with moss in the winter to keep it warmer.
Eats tree buds, bark, leaves and fungi.
Lives in dens underground.
Can live in parks, cities and woodland.
Good at leaping and running along tree branches.
Can write using a stick.
Normally lives for 3–4 years.
Curls its tail around its body as it sleeps, like a blanket.
Hides food supplies in the ground for winter.
Changes colour when it is angry.
Finds its food supplies by sense of smell.

Appendix T6F4

Fact file: Song thrush

Has brown plumage and a speckled chest.
Kills and eats snails by smashing their shells against a stone.
Lives in woodland, parks and gardens.
Eats bananas in the summer.
Song thrush eggs are sky-blue in colour with black spots.
Song thrushes build their nest in a bush or a tree.
Is scared of the dark.
Has pink legs and a brown beak.
Can live to be fifteen years old.
Farmers do not like song thrushes, as they eat their soft fruit crops.
A song thrush is 23 cm long.
Song thrushes repeat their songs up to four times.

Appendix T6F5

Buzzard fact file

- Buzzards prefer living in hills, wooded valleys and mountains.
- A buzzard eats small mammals and insects.
- Its favourite food is rabbit.
- It has sharp claws called talons.
- A buzzard has a very sharp beak for eating its prey.
- A buzzard makes a 'kiew, kiew' sound when it calls.
- It hovers in the air, looking for movements in the grass before catching its prey.
- Buzzards build large nests in trees.
- Buzzards are fearsome hunters.
- Buzzards can swim.
- Buzzards eat bananas in the summer.
- Buzzards have very poor eyesight.
- A buzzard is the size of a robin.
- Its wings are very wide and have long black feathers at the tips.
- Buzzards have yellow legs and browny-grey feathers.

Appendix T6F6

Buzzard fact file

- Buzzards prefer living in hills, wooded valleys, mountains and coastal areas.
- Buzzards eat small mammals, carrion and insects.
- A buzzard makes a distinctive 'kiew, kiew' sound.
- It has sharp claws called talons and a hooked beak.
- It hovers in the air, looking for movements below before diving to catch its prey.
- Buzzards build large nests in trees or on cliff ledges.
- Buzzards are fearsome hunters and their favourite food is rabbit.
- They use warm air thermals to soar high into the sky.
- Buzzards almost died out before the First World War.
- Buzzards can swim.
- Buzzards eat bananas in the summer.
- Buzzards have very poor eyesight.
- A buzzard is the size of a robin.
- Its wings are very wide and have long, finger-like black feathers at the tips.
- Buzzards have yellow legs and browny-grey speckled plumage.

Appendix T6F7

Mole fact file

- Moles are insectivores, meaning they just eat insects.
- Moles have tiny eyes and poor eyesight.
- Their front feet are very large and used for burrowing.
- A mole's strongest sense is its sense of touch.
- Baby moles are called pups.
- The main predator of a mole is the owl.
- Moles can dig tunnels many metres long.
- The piles of soil made from digging such long tunnels are called molehills.
- A mole's saliva contains a poison that paralyses the earthworms it preys upon when it bites them.
- Moles like to live under grassy fields, lawns and pastures.

Appendix T6J1

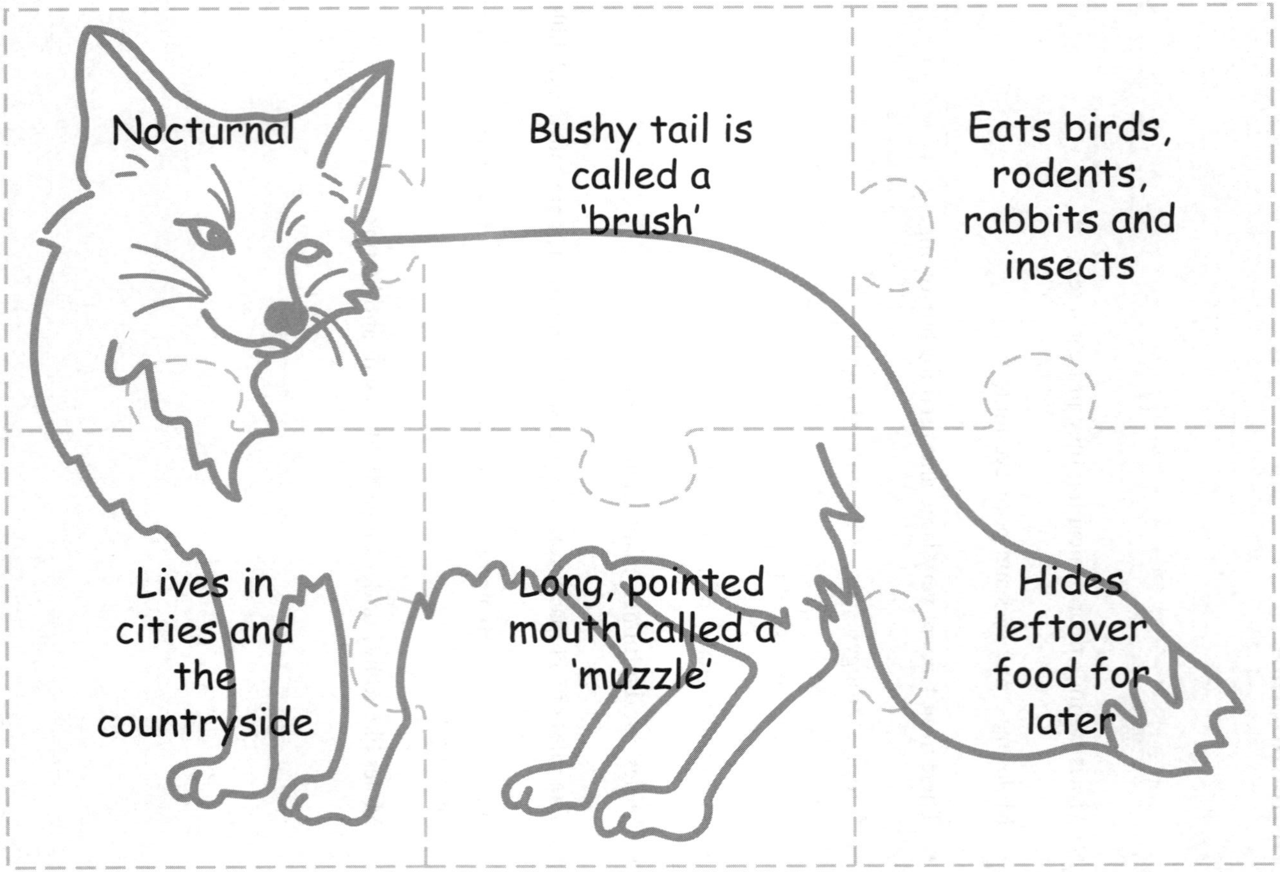

Nocturnal
Bushy tail is called a 'brush'
Eats birds, rodents, rabbits and insects
Lives in cities and the countryside
Long, pointed mouth called a 'muzzle'
Hides leftover food for later

Appendix T6J2

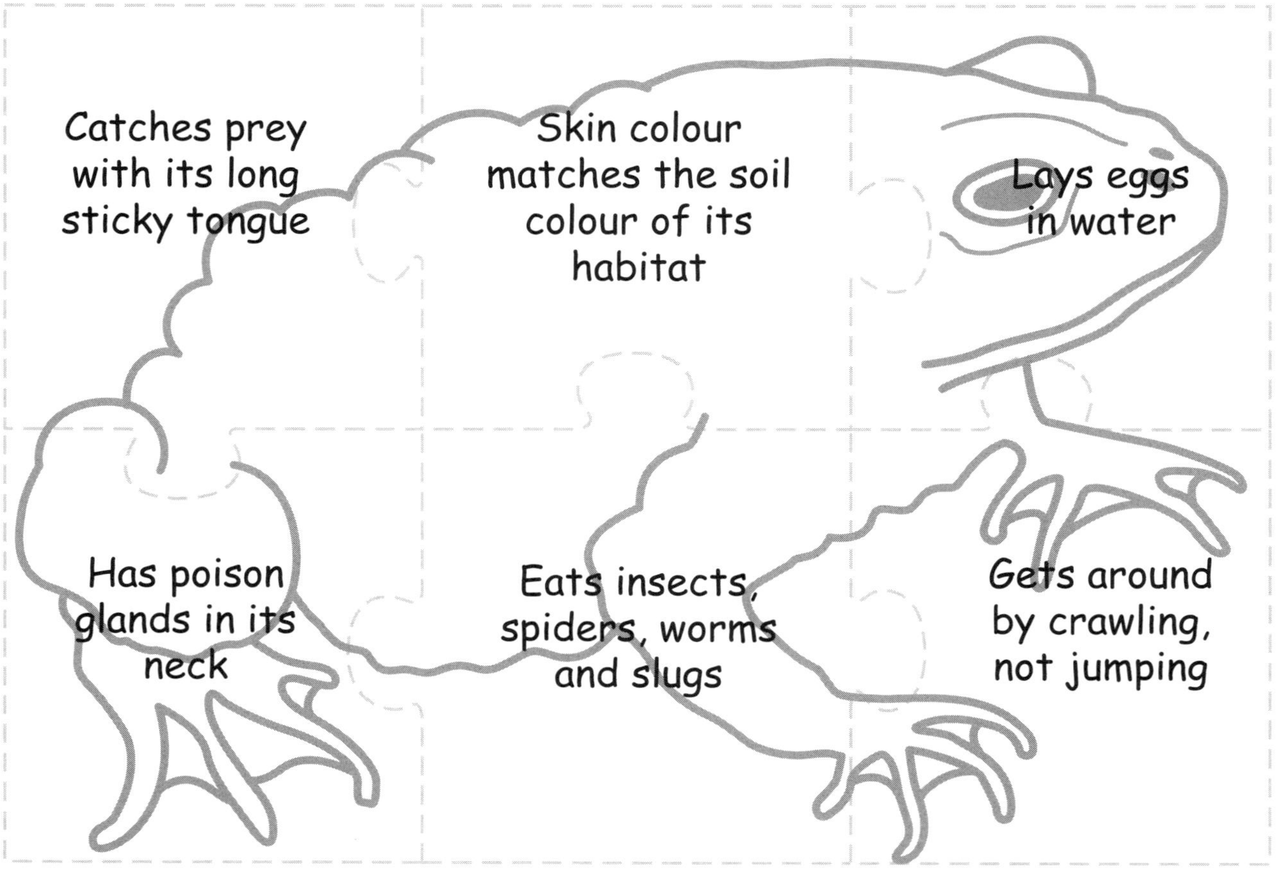

Catches prey with its long sticky tongue
Skin colour matches the soil colour of its habitat
Lays eggs in water
Has poison glands in its neck
Eats insects, spiders, worms and slugs
Gets around by crawling, not jumping

Appendix T6J3

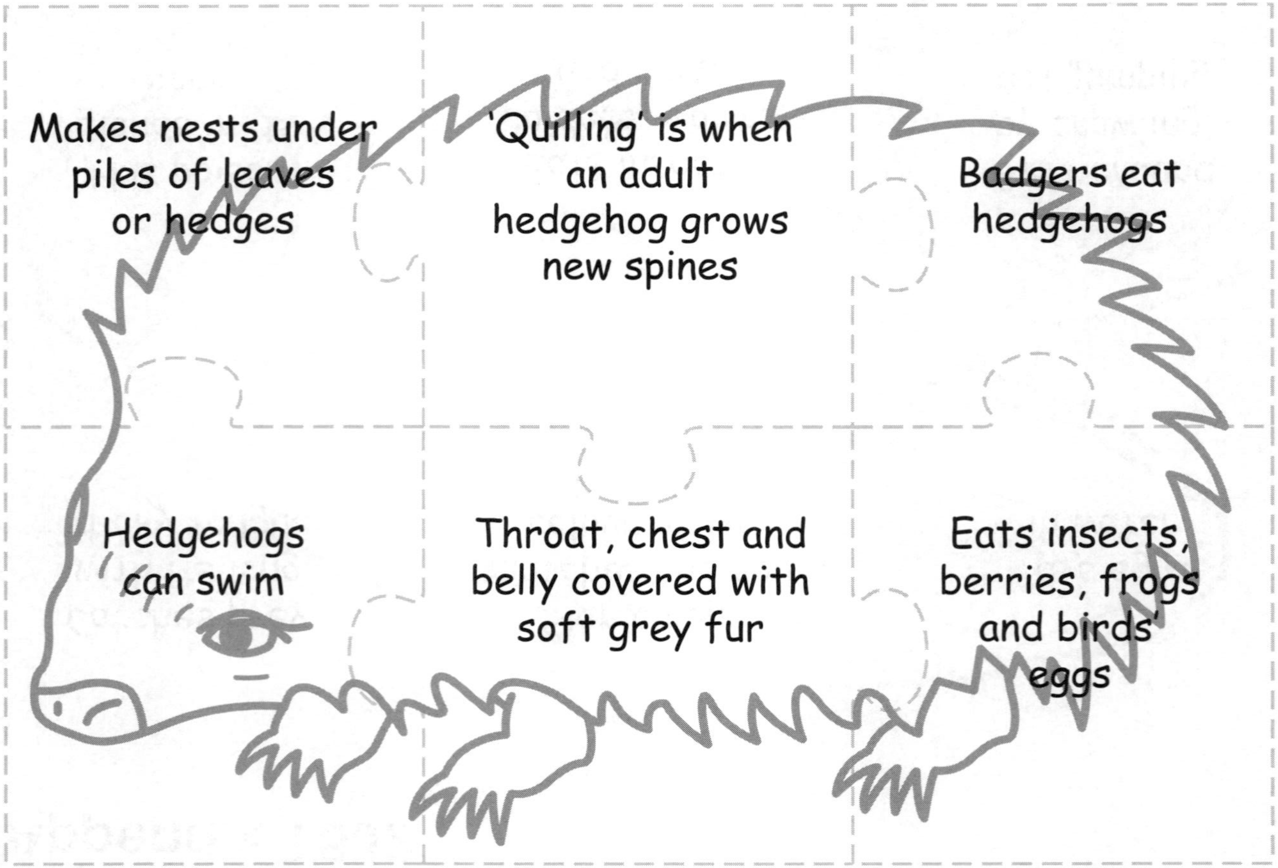
Makes nests under piles of leaves or hedges
'Quilling' is when an adult hedgehog grows new spines
Badgers eat hedgehogs
Hedgehogs can swim
Throat, chest and belly covered with soft grey fur
Eats insects, berries, frogs and birds' eggs

Appendix T6J4

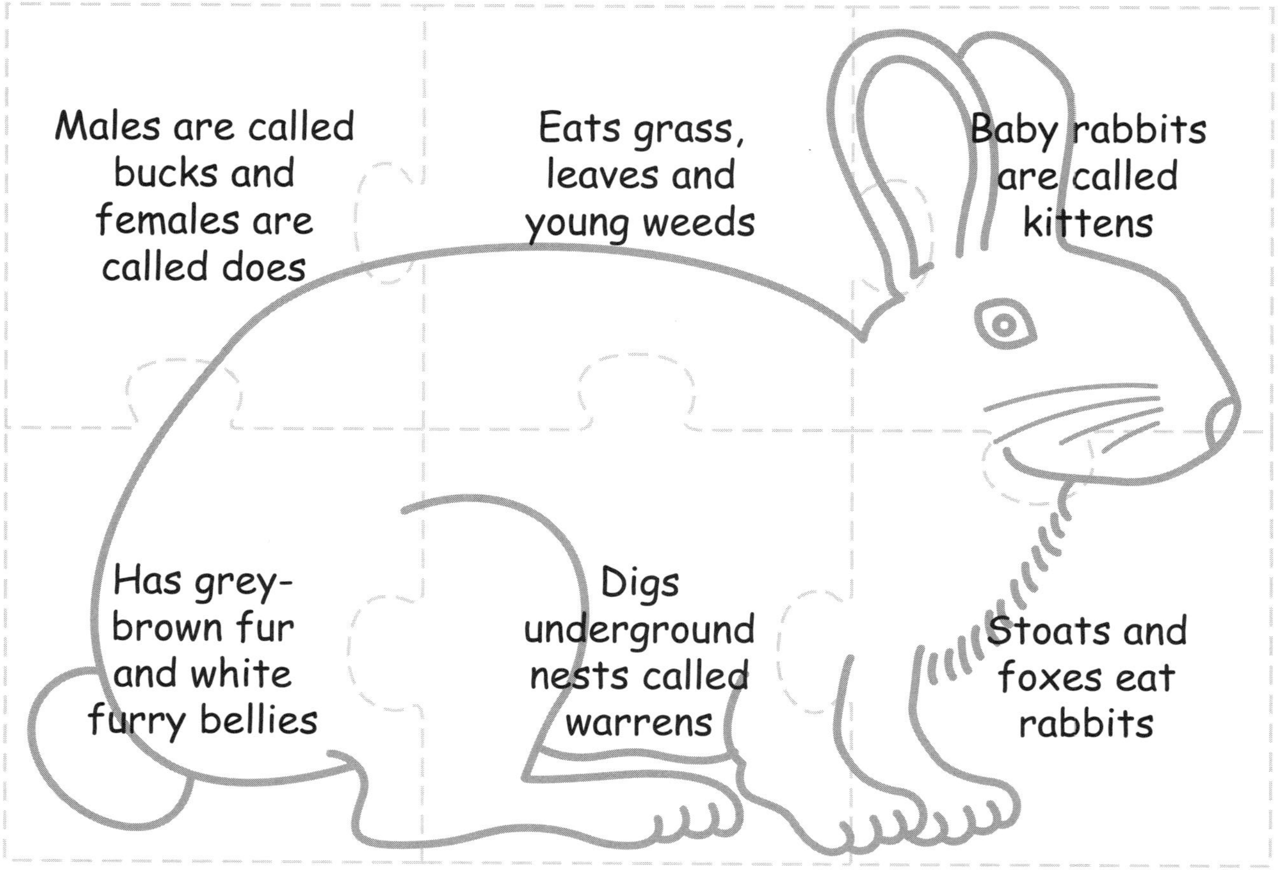

Males are called bucks and females are called does
Eats grass, leaves and young weeds
Baby rabbits are called kittens
Has grey-brown fur and white furry bellies
Digs underground nests called warrens
Stoats and foxes eat rabbits

Appendix T6L1

Hello!

Can you see us?

We can see you, so you'd better not be silly!

Don't worry, we're just some animals who live here. We saw some of you at playtime last week, and decided to teach you more about who we are and the other animals that live round here.

But first, you'll have to work out what we are! Once you've done that, we'll teach you a bit more about us . . . Have fun!

Your woodland friends

Appendix T6L2

Welcome back! Isn't it a lovely day for being outside?

We thought that today we'd try to show you some more of the animals that live around here. We're quite a shy bunch, and some of us are even nocturnal, so I'm afraid we won't just come and sit in front of you.

But we've made some jigsaws for you to find, and we'll be watching from the trees to make sure you find all the pieces.

Do you think you can use the information you discover to make a poster that teaches your friends all about us?

Good luck!

Your woodland friends

Appendix T6L3

Hello again!

Even if you looked really carefully, you wouldn't be able to find us today. Why? Because we're hiding over the fence!

Unfortunately, we're not playing a game. We were told yesterday by a badger that a new animal is thinking of moving into our woods. We've heard lots of rumours about this animal, and we're not sure if they're going to make a good neighbour for us all or not. We've written down everything that we know about it in a special fact pack, and we've hidden one for you to find.

Can you take a look and decide if they'll make a good neighbour or not? You can leave a note for us out here.

Yours worriedly,

Your woodland friends

Appendix T6L4

Phew, what a lucky escape!

The rabbits in particular were very relieved that we turned the buzzard away. We felt a bit guilty, but we also feel a lot safer!

Now we've got another puzzle for you to help us with. Yesterday morning, an animal that we have never seen before arrived in the woods. He was quite scared at first, but then he told us that he was lost. He was exhausted from trying to find his way home, so he's still sleeping on a pile of leaves now!

Can you help us work out what animal he is, and whether he could live here with us? Is this the right habitat? Will he be able to find the food he needs? It seems mean to send him away when he might fit in perfectly. And perhaps you might be able to help us make a nest for him to recover in, where we can keep an eye on him.

Thanks again,

Your woodland friends

Appendix T6L5

Hello again!

This will be the last time that you hear from us for a while, but we have one more favour to ask.

Brian the mole (did we tell you his name last week?) decided to stay after all, and he had a really good idea. He said that there might be lots of other animals like him who have to move to new areas because they get lost, or lose their habitat. He thought that it would be really useful if new arrivals like him could find out about the other animals already living here. We had a meeting of all the animals, and decided that we needed you to help us make a sort of report book, which has pictures and information about all the different creatures that live here. You could also use it to teach the other children in your school all about us.

Perhaps you could leave it under the tree when it's finished so that we can take a look? We promise to wash our paws and beaks before we turn the pages!

Your woodland friends

References

Bereiter, C. and Scardamalia, M. (1987) *The Psychology of Written Composition*. Hillsdale, NJ: Erlbaum.

Carver, C. S. (2003) Pleasure as a sign you can attend to something else: placing positive feelings within a general model of affect. *Cognition and Emotion*, 17(2): 241–261.

Claxton, G. (2002) *Building Learning Power: helping young people become better learners*. Bristol: TLO Limited.

Corbett, P. (2008) *Storytelling*. London: The National Strategies.

Craft, Anna (2001) 'Little C' creativity. In Craft, A., Jeffrey, B. and Leibling, M., *Creativity in Education*. London: Continuum International.

Crumpler, T. P. (2005) The role of educational drama in the composing processes of young writers. *Research in Drama Education*, 10(3): 357–363.

Department for Education and Skills (2006) *Primary Framework for Literacy and Mathematics*. Norwich: DfES Publications.

Dewey, J. (1938) *Experience and Education*. New York: Collier Books.

Dismore, H. and Bailey, R. (2005) 'If only': outdoor and adventurous activities and generalised academic development. *Journal of Adventure Education and Outdoor Learning*, 5(1): 9–20.

Forestry Commission for Scotland (2005) Education strategy. *Woods for Learning*. Forestry Commission for Scotland, Edinburgh.

Gardner, H. (1993) *Frames of Mind: the theory of multiple intelligences*, 2nd edn. New York: Basic Books.

Grahn, P., Martensoon, F., Lindblad, B., Nilsoon, P. and Ekman, A. (1997) *Ute pa dagis. Stad and Land, mr. 145 [Outdoor Daycare, City and Country]*. Hasselholm, Sweden: Norra Skane Offset.

Hopwood, I. (2011) Evaluating the impact of Forest School sessions on writing outcomes for low-achieving children. Master's thesis submitted to Bath Spa University, Continuing Professional Development Department, February 2011.

Margerison, A. (1996) Self-esteem: its effects on the development and learning of children with EBD. *Support for Learning*, 11(4): 176–179.

Murray, R. and O'Brien, L. (2005) *Such Enthusiasm – a Joy to See: an evaluation of Forest School in England*. London: New Economics Foundation.

Mygind, E. (2007) A comparison between children's physical activity levels at school and learning in an outdoor environment. *Journal of Adventure Education and Outdoor Learning*, 7(2): 161–176.

O'Brien, L. (2004) *A Sort of Magical Place: people's experiences of woodlands in Northwest and Southeast England*. Farnham: Forest Research.

Pilsbury, R. (2008) *Forest School Briefing Paper*. Wolverhampton: Wolverhampton City Council.

Rickinson, M., Dillon, J., Teamey, K., Morris, M., Young Choi, M., Sanders, D. and Benefield, P. (2004) *A Review of the Research on Outdoor Learning*. London: National Foundation for Educational Research and King's College London.

Scheuer, N., De La Cruz, M., Pozo, J. I., Huarte, M. F. and Sola, G. (2006) The mind is not a black box: children's ideas about the writing process. *Learning and Instruction*, 16: 72–85.

Vygotsky, L.S. (1978) *Mind and Society: the development of higher psychological processes*. Cambridge, MA: Harvard University Press.

Waite, S. (2007) Memories are made of this: some reflections on outdoor learning and recall. *Education 3–13*, 35(4): 333–347.

Waller, T. (2007) 'The trampoline tree and the swamp monster with 18 heads': outdoor play in the Foundation Stage and the Foundation Phase. *Education 3–13*, 35(4): 393–407.

Williams-Siegfredsen, J. (2005) *The Competent Child: developing children's skills and confidence using the outdoor environment – a Danish perspective*. Paper presented at the BERA Annual Conference.